WILDLIFE
WANDERINGS

First published in Great Britain in 2020
Copyright © David Bailey

British Library Cataloguing-in-Publication Data
A CIP record for this title is available from the British Library

ISBN 978 0 85704 352 8

Halsgrove
Halsgrove House,
Ryelands Business Park,
Bagley Road, Wellington, Somerset TA21 9PZ
Tel: 01823 653777   Fax: 01823 216796
email: sales@halsgrove.com

Part of the Halsgrove group of companies
Information on all Halsgrove titles is available at:
www.halsgrove.com

Printed and bound in India by Parksons Graphics Ltd

WILDLIFE
WANDERINGS

David Bailey

HALSGROVE

CONTENTS

FOREWORD

From my recall as a young child, one of my earliest memories is being very aware of the outside world and its inhabitants. The colour and shape of a very simple plant such as a dandelion still evokes in me during my later years a sense of wonderment. As I walk my dogs across the Purbeck hills here in Dorset in early spring with all of nature starting to come out of its winter slumber, you sense the awakening of everything around you beginning to grow with birds and animals beginning to establish their territories and the flora and fauna stirring out of its winter dormancy. As spring progresses and the climate warms up there is a burst of activity throughout the whole of nature. I've been lucky during my childhood to have experienced sights of elvers – juvenile eels – running up my local river to carry out their next stage of life, salmon swimming up river to their spawning gravels to lay their eggs which is rarer now to see due to overfishing. Water voles so common that they were everywhere in large rivers and small streams. Curlews coming onto our heathland to breed along with plovers both which such evocative calls, also snipe drumming as part of their mating flight.

All of this is becoming less common to experience especially for young children due to the way that society has expanded and with our approach and appreciation of the environment we live in. The freedom I experienced when I was young such as going out all day immersing myself into this fascinating outside world is one most youngsters will not partake in. It's very difficult to get across to the younger generation that just standing on a hill with swifts swooping just a foot above your head catching insects with the sound of the air rushing through their wings is so exciting and memorable. Walking through an area of rough wild water meadows and pushing a dog fox out and then a vixen shortly after from a clump of tall grass, to then go over and find in this clump a litter of thirteen fox cubs with

their eyes not yet open is an extremely rare happening but one that my friends and I as children will never forget. One of the things as a child I would love to have owned was a camera to record some of these experiences, but all I carried was a pair of ex German U Boat binoculars to observe the goings on of life in the wild.

As you go through life of course, if you still maintain an interest in the outside environment you maybe specialise and research particular forms of life. With more leisure time most people can often become very knowledgeable on the subject they pursue and can actually become quite expert in finding new evidence and information on that particular subject.

The main thing to take away from my ramblings is that it is not too late to get out into nature and become one with it. No matter where you live, even in the heart of a big city, nature and its inhabitants are still around for you to observe and appreciate. Maybe circumstances mean that this may not even be possible due to mobility problems and all you have are your memories and what comes into your life is via the media. Well, reading my words must mean that you have bought this book or thinking of purchasing it. Do so please! I met the author, David Bailey, three years ago or so due to him approaching our museum setup here in Kimmeridge and having a temporary exhibition of his wildlife photography. It actually turned out he reminded me that we had met years before when he delivered to my house an air compressor to enable me to carry out using air tools to clean my fossils. This was more than twenty-five years ago when I lived not in Kimmeridge as I do now but at my previous address in Wimborne. In those years succeeding God knows what he has done and when he started his now successful career as a wildlife photographer. For those who don't know him, he resides at the moment in mid Wales in a cottage with only a wood burner for heat and lives on hardly any food! Any visitors don't normally stay too long because of his primitive living conditions! His life he has chosen as a wildlife photographer is a very precarious one due to the fact that it will not make him extremely rich in money but makes him in my eyes one of the richest in what he experiences. To go out in the field and obtain the sort of images he is after comes through often months of waiting in all weathers to get the shot he is after. Doing so he has to have the knowledge to know where to find his subject, how it interacts and lots of other things that only come through patience and experience. It's very easy to flick through the pages and see these incredible images of wildlife in their natural habitat but not appreciate the time it takes to achieve the perfect photo. It must be remembered that none of these images are controlled or altered to get that final shot. I love seeing them because I also have seen similar occurrences through my life but mine are only recorded in my memory.

All I can say is thanks to people such as David, we can appreciate nature in all is forms by reading this book and inspiring us to all into the great outdoors and value our amazing surroundings and the wildlife that inhabits it.

Dr Steve Etches MBE

INTRODUCTION

Wildlife Wanderings is my second published book. I consider myself very fortunate to have been able to write as at the age of four years old I could neither read nor talk, born with an extremely high roof to my mouth, nearly a cleft palate and misaligned sticky out teeth. All I could verbally make was a series of noises.

Fourteen years of speech therapy followed with Miss Hamilton at Odstock Hospital (now named Salisbury Hospital) and suffering dental work for the same number of years. I owe much that I have achieved to the people involved, although to this day there are words I still cannot pronounce such as 'belligerent'; instead I automatically say an equivalent word without having to think about it. More annoying though is that I simply love Italian food, could eat it for breakfast, lunch, supper, grow fat and happy. But give me a restaurant menu with 'Tortellini' there is no way can I pronounce it so I choose something else which I can or prod the menu with my finger!

Something that has always stuck in my mind was Miss Hamilton telling my mother that I would get through life but not achieve much and in more recent years a relation informed me I would never make a success at photography. Persons making statements like that only serve to spur me on, more determined than ever.

Always a loner since my childhood, never a people person, I would sooner take myself off into the woods to play and watch animals on my own. Stealthily climbing a tree to find a bushy red tail of a squirrel hanging in my face is a wonderful childhood memory. My father, Chris with his two-fingered-on-top-of-rolled-tongue whistle which was so piercingly loud the sparrows would fall off their perches in fright, would be the only reason I ever returned home. Being whistled to informed me of my mother's burnt offerings or soggy heavy cakes were ready to be consumed, hence spending my days out photographing on my own is pretty much normal for me although I do miss those whistles.

Obsessed is not the word I would use to describe myself when it comes to photography – more like bloody minded, persistent never knowing when to give up. Over the years I have seen many call themselves 'Wildlife Photographers' not being able to make it pay then turning to so called easy money, wedding photography, something although I have been asked to photograph I could never undertake as I would certainly fall out with the mother-in-law for a start!

In the early days of my photographic career I also photographed events working with members of the Royal Family, well known sports stars etc but realised I had to specialise, and because animals have such a hold on me that humans never will it was a no brainer.

To sell your work besides producing quality images, means finding your market. In the past I have literally stood on street corners at markets in all types of weather. Once my card spinner was blown over with hundreds of cards being chased by passers-by down the street.

Craft fairs, agriculture shows, sheep dog trials, food festivals I've exhibited at them all. It's part of my apprenticeship and I'm still learning. Over the years your audience changes as does the economic environment, not allowing for different types of people who are interested enough to purchase any prints.

However, I found my niche in presenting talks with slideshows. People describe me as an entertainer, explaining the stories behind the images. By captivating the audience I have ready-made customers to buy my work. Little do they know of my speech impediment!

People's goodwill in helping me has been simply amazing and has formed a large part of any success I have achieved. Good examples are Dr Jane Goodall and Bill Oddie, both so kind as to have contributed the blurb for this book. I met Bill during the filming of a documentary called 'Plumbing the Depths', thanks to the kindness of a good friend, Pinewood-based director Pete Sheppard who had invited both myself and Bill to the location at The Etches Collection Fossil Museum at Kimmeridge, Dorset. Bill was filmed

Eric Ashby Lens

with various people talking about the art of collecting fossils and I took an interview with world famous fossil collector Steve Etches chatting about his father who was a photographer. It was two days filming and Bill had brought along his close friend Lynn Hazel, a wildlife sculptress. Early the second morning I had decided to look for adders on a bank not far from the hotel where Bill and Lynn were staying so Lynn asked if she could join me in the hunt. Bill decided to stay in bed and slept on which was just as well as we could not find one adder due to the undergrowth having grown more than I expected since my last visit. I dropped Lynn back at the hotel who obviously told Bill what happened. Later arriving on location, Bill's words to me, 'sorry Dave I forgot to put the snakes out'!!!!

The late Eric Ashby is a source of inspiration to me. Living near the Red Shoot pub at Linwood in the New Forest, his camera techniques to film and photograph wildlife were very much the forerunner to any wildlife footage you see today. For instance building an artificial badger set in his garden he captured images and built up an understanding of this creature never seen before. Foxes were another great love of his with two books published called, *The Secret Life of The New Forest* (1989) and *My Life with Foxes* (2000). Reading these books gives you great understanding of one man's genuine care for the natural world. I have been very fortunate to have been asked to Eric's old cottage now extended and modernised, but the old artificial badger set has been reconstructed and now is in use once again by furry residents. More recently I very carefully handled one of Eric's old camera lenses and while standing there with film-making history in my hands I could not help thinking what a privilege this was, what had been spied through this lens and wishing I had been beside the man while he filmed.

With very few exceptions all my photographs are wild animals. The only time I would ever consider going to a captive venue is for something rare and extinct in the wild such as the Pere David deer at Margam Park or the Welsh beaver yet (at the time of writing) to be released into the wild. It's a challenge to capture a special image of a wild animal, waiting and watching which means sitting still for hours on end. In this photograph the temperature was -5°C with wind chill taking temperatures down to -12°C. Nine hours in the hide and with so many hours sitting waiting hardly moving, some may ask about the call of nature. I have two flasks, you can work out the rest!!!!!!

The Good, The Bad and The Hysterical pretty much sums up events that happen while I attempt to work as a photographer. The Good describes all the fantastic wildlife I record. The Bad, is the side of my work which I don't advertise much, finding snared badgers, witnessing hare coursing, Court witness to crime etc. With The Hysterical, one story stands out above all others. My partner Yvonne I'm sure (or hopeful) she will agree is a bit of a townie having grown up and lived her life in the Poole area of Dorset and had never witnessed the deer rut. Hence one October I took her into the New Forest in the hope she would see this magnificent sight for the first time in her life. But my timing was not good, a Saturday and the start of the school's half term. There were more people in the Forest than attending the FA Cup Final. Eventually at around four in the afternoon we did find a quiet area with a group of about fifteen fallow does quietly grazing. We watched them for about five minutes when from our right a lurcher ran past to the deer, split off one doe which disappeared at high speed with the dog chasing. It was poachers with no sign of the dog handler, but I did manage a head shot of the lurcher as it passed and found it had a very distinctive collar. I immediately phoned the police. The call handler took my details

Frozen in Hide

Len Witt

and location informing me she would pass the report on. Imagine my surprise when ten minutes later my phone rang, and a voice on the other end said, 'Hampshire Police Wildlife Crime Unit where are you, we are here?' Being beside a small river that ran down into the Forest from the main road where the boys in blue were parked I told them if they followed the river downstream we would meet. No more than five minutes later two breathless uniforms came running. They had driven on a rough track into the Forest and parked just upstream from us.

Looking at the screen on the back of my camera I showed the picture of the lurcher with said collar. 'Right let's try and find the dog and handler' they exclaimed, 'it's not often we get a red-hot tip like this and with photographic proof', and off we charged. Yvonne on the other hand was struggling. Made of quite stern stuff she would battle through most things but she had a chest infection and could not

keep up with us so she decided to walk back to the police Land Rover and wait as she had a fold-up chair to rest in. The three of us crossed the river and searched the woods to find an illicit camp with twelve youths drinking, eating and with an open fire (which is illegal in the Forest) but no dog. At this point it was starting to get progressively quite dark. I was becoming concerned about Yvonne not feeling well and sitting in the dark with fallow bucks bellowing all around her as by this time of evening they were really vocal. I left the camp on my own and retraced our steps, having to cross the river in the dark to reach Yvonne beside the Land Rover on the other side. We had to wait for the police. After half an hour it was pitch black. I was starting to wonder if indeed the boys remembered where they had parked; if they did not return what should I do? Massive splash, there standing in the middle of the river was one policeman up to his groin in the water. Not realising how wide it was he had tried jumping and landed short. His colleague standing on the bank had a better idea, took off his radio, and threw it to us followed by his stab jacket. He then took a run up, slipped on the bank and ended up sitting in the river. Soaked, it's a good job they had a sense of humour, especially when Yvonne who up to that point had been speechless, I believe because she was laughing so much, informed the soggy policemen there was a bridge no more than 20 metres away!

The story still did not end there as the police offered a lift back to my car parked beside the main road. Myself and Yvonne sitting in the back were thrown about like ragdolls as the officer driving was not messing about in the dark. Mud, ruts, ditches, going like the clappers we zoomed through the lot, only for the driver to announce as he was desperately hanging onto the steering wheel, he was not used to driving this vehicle as his normal car was written off the previous night after being rammed by poachers!

Later that evening while driving back to Yvonne's house, she turned to me and said 'well you certainly know how show a girl a good time out on a Saturday night!'.

If you are wondering what happened to the lurcher, neither the dog which had been stolen from nearby Chandlers Ford or its handler was ever found.

I have never explained or been asked why I'm naming my books using Wanderings or Wanderer! It's in memory of my grandfather Len Witt, an old New Forester. Back in 1958 a book written by Juliette de Bairacli Levy called *Wanderers in the New Forest* was first published and it featured my grandfather and his way of life, even written in his local dialect.

My mother's family came from generations of New Foresters. Her parents lived originally at Home Farm, Blissford, before her father died when mother was only five years old. Later gran married Len and moved to Windy Ridge at Frogham, hence Len was always granddad to me.

Len was a local character. All his life he ran the famous New Forest ponies out on the heaths, owned a handful of cows, had fields of strawberries that all the family helped pick during the summer, taking weekly pony trap rides to Southampton which was a good 20 miles away to sell his goods, even making Christmas holly wreaths which he sold in the capital by travelling up by train from Brockenhurst. It must have been an awesome experience for someone who used to travel by horse, to sell on the streets of London – a journey he only stopped making after he was robbed one year.

Dolly the cow reflected Len's character. Gentle yet occasionally stubborn, she often spent nights in an old wooden shed in the yard and was led by Len with a length of binder twine tied round her horns out onto the Forest most mornings to be let loose to graze returning in the evenings to her cosy shed.

One memory of Len that will always stick with me is that you could hear him coming miles away. His hobnail boots seemed enormous to me with what seemed to be six-inch nails driven into the bottom of the leather soles. They would go clooop, clooop clooop – the sound of metal raining down on tarmacadam. On meeting a neighbour, he would stop to talk – or shout, as he was almost deaf. Life was never quiet with him about.

Towards the end of Len's life, I can remember him chatting about old times, sitting in the parlour of his mud-walled cottage in front the open fire with cast iron kettle hanging over for hot water. My father and I were two of the few remaining people who could understand what he was saying in such a rich local New Forest language.

I often read *Wanderers in the New Forest*. It takes me back to simple happy times and I can slip straight back into that dialect. My lovely old Welsh neighbours in the Brecon Beacons, Will and Jackie could not understand the book on loaning it to them because of the way it had been written.

In another throw back to my New Forest roots and grandfather Len, *Wildlife Wanderings* is split into the four seasons. Three of the chapters are named in old New Forest dialect due to the kindness of the New Forest Heritage Centre for their research in finding these words and phrases. However there was no reference to Autumn to be found so I have used the old English word of Haerfest. Each chapter contains images with short stories of wildlife you can expect to see during those particular seasons. All the stories are written what I term as fresh, written within a day of capturing the image while the story is fresh in my mind.

Hence my reason for the book and chapter naming, and although Len's way of life may have long gone, I'm going to carry on my wanderings, recording life as I see it hopefully for your enjoyment.

David Bailey

Len on Horseback

SPRING-BIRD

William H. Cope, *A Glossary of Hampshire Words and Phrases* (1883). Spring-bird is the New Forest word for Ray's wagtail because it appears around the time for sowing barley (spring time).

The season of new life, foliage sprouting out fresh green shoots, and animals and birds in love showing their affections to their loved ones for the sole purpose of bringing the next generation into this world. With longer daylight hours with a touch of warmth as the rawness of winter fades. Spring is a wonderful time of year.

It is my busiest time of all the seasons. From March to mid-June if it is a nice day I'm out happily snapping as romance is in the air and those creatures who are normally shy and retiring can drop their guard and the new born are not yet worldly wise.

I am always being asked what is my favourite subject. Although I love all wildlife, the hare is indeed my favourite, characters without question with spring the best time to watch this marvellous animal. The 'mad March hare' syndrome is at its height with the males chasing females. Because the crops are low, even on a grassy field with just four inches of growth a fully-grown hare can lay so flat you will not see it, which so far as predators are concerned is the whole idea. I have witnessed a hare relaxing in the sun on short grass near my hide; on hearing people talking while walking a nearby footpath, the hare spread its front and hind legs, sank down and disappeared from sight.

Bahh Humbugs!!

Wild boar – 'aren't they dangerous?' Apparently, that's what people keep telling me although I disagree: boar behaviour is very much like that of adders, an attack would be the last resort and would only normally happen through your own stupidity or being very unlucky as both species would rather run/slither away and hide.

Early spring is a good time to seek wild boar before grass grows high and bushes become heavy with leaves, affording the animals shelter to hide. They do this well as I found out on my first visit to the Forest of Dean, being greeted in the dim light of early morning by three hairy shapes resembling tiny elephants without the trunks shuffling across the road nose to tail in front my car forcing me to hit the brakes. That encounter lulled me into falsely thinking it was going to be easy to find and photograph these beasts. What could be harder! Parking near a pond in the heart of the forest, loading gear on my back and camera in hand I skirted the end of the pond meeting an elderly couple sweetly holding hands, out for their early morning stroll. Always talk to the locals is my motto and in doing so had a lovely, friendly, informative conversation with these two old love birds who had been walking the area for years and directed me to the best location to find the boars. Wishing the couple a pleasant day and following their instructions I retraced my steps past my car. I climbed up a massive wooded hill with broadleaf trees on the lower slopes and a fir plantation further up with a flat plateau of thick gorse, ringed once again with broadleaf trees.

Truth is that you can hardly miss where boar have been with evidence everywhere. Either that or it's a drunk out of control in a digger! Total destruction with upturned roots and divots greeted me in the area surrounding the edge of the plateau. Witnessing the devastation

I can fully understand local villagers keeping their garden gates well and truly closed, protecting unblemished lawns and prized flower borders.

Finding fresh soil in the chaotic earthworks gave a clue that my quarry had been there during the last few hours. I set off tiptoeing round the edge of the plateau, being ever so careful not to tread on a twig or any other matter that might crack and give my presence away.

As the hours ticked by and the sun rose high in the sky I was no longer tiptoeing, just flagging in the heat. With no signs of my piggy foes I called it a day. Feeling despondent I stumbled down the hillside to accidently meet a gentleman with camera not far from my car. Greeting each other I asked if he had seen boar; yes came the reply I've been photographing them all morning and he described where they had been. On hearing I had not seen one he offered to show me a sow with piglets. We walked no more than one hundred metres when through the trees a big hairy ear was pointed out to me. The ear was attached to a sow who had about six piglets. My friendly stranger backed off to leave me hidden behind a small fir tree to one side of a track. Within minutes the sow came onto the track with piglets trailing some distance behind. From my position I could get a clear shot of the sow, click went my camera, immediately sow froze, click, sow looked, click, sow ran into thick fir cover followed closely by piglets.

That was my first meeting with such a dangerous animal and I was up for the challenge to capture close up and detailed images, so a week after my first visit I returned.

Early morning after checking round the base, I climbed the same hill and as before found fresh soil turned over on the edge of the plateau. It was then I disturbed a sow snuffling around at the edge of the thick gorse. Grunting, she shot off quicker than the Japanese Bullet Train. Sadly, I thought that was my chance gone, but how wrong I was. After walking a few yards I found a track into the gorse and there at the far end were the four piglets – nicknamed humbugs due to their stripy back, resembling the well-known sweet.

As the piglets were busy grovelling around in the earth and some distance away none had seen me, I dived flat to the ground in the middle of the track, removed my backpack using it as a camera rest and waited for the young boar who were slowly but ever so surely working their way down the track towards me.

Patience IS a virtue, as lying so close to the ground the boar had to be close to capture a good clean image using my 500mm lens. Closer they came, being intent on juvenile behaviour and the rooting out of grubs. Oh, to be innocent again. The feeling of not needing to worry about anything must be lovely, something I forgot about years ago, unlike the young boar who came within touching distance before realising that something was not quite normal. But by then I had captured my images.

Military Bird

Like a well-planned clandestine military operation my written instructions were as follows: someone will meet you on the A3** road at the layby with the bus shelter by the crossroads in the village of S******* on Salisbury Plain at 06.30 hrs. My mission, should I choose to accept it, was to photograph Great Bustards.

Arriving early at 06.10 hrs an unmarked sinister black Range Rover appeared out of the gloom. An unseen face from the driver's seat shouted out the open passenger window, 'Are you Dave?' I shouted back 'yes'. Follow me' the voice replied. Taking the north road out of the village, eventually turning left and down a track to a farm yard where the Range Rover skidded to a sudden stop, I parked beside expecting to see a camo-clothed figure with blacked out face possibly carrying an automatic rifle emerging. Instead and maybe with some air of disappointment on my behalf, a rather jolly rounded person fell out of the door and introduced himself, pointing out there could be a problem. 'What no Great Bustards', I replied with some degree of alarm. I was instructed to put my gear into a waiting Land Rover and come into a building where a Great Bustard fancy dress outfit was handed to me. 'Put this on as we don't want the birds to associate with humans'. My thoughts were that humans would not want to associate with me either wearing this!

The old saying is the proof is in the pudding. It was the lekking season and the reason for my timed visit, so if an amorous cock bird started chasing me, I would be the first one convinced that the disguise worked. We jumped into the battered old Land Rover and started off up the valley onto the Army ranges when the said problem became evident – a flood. Many place names in Wiltshire contain the word Bourne meaning river which is not there all the time, just present during autumn and winter after heavy rainfall when the river suddenly appears from the chalk down lands. This indeed was our problem but as luck would have it the water level had dropped from the previous day and we could drive through, JUST!

After all these adventures I arrived on site and was shown into a hide with the resident bustards showing no interest in my glamorous outfit, while my companion, who I felt did not look quite so fetching as moi, grabbed a bucket of feed to put out. He ventured past the hide with bucket in hand to be met by one huge cock bird. Thirty seconds of pandemonium followed. Imagine if you can, man in bustard outfit, one real bustard trying its best to get head in bucket, grab bucket or literally bite the hand feeding it, to the pretend-bustard yells of 'stay right there, get off, leave me alone' followed by hasty retreat back past my hide.

I was quite pleased to be left to my own devices in the hide, needing time to recover from what had been a quite eventful morning and it was not even 07.30 hrs. Time was on my side although weather conditions were far from perfect. The bustards put on their fanciful dance, gizzards blown up like a balloon, feathers ruffled in display with quick 90-degree rotation movements. I was not alone as one of these beautiful birds came to visit me five times to have a chat about all the world's problems through the hide window, although I did not step outside just in case my fancy costume worked!

Cheesy Goats

Cheddar Gorge is one of the UK's natural splendours formed by meltwater during the past 1.2 million years and found in the Mendip Hills of Somerset. It is famous for its caves in which have been found remains of ancient man and which are popular for cave diving. The most famous product of the area is the celebrated cheese, which traditionally had to be made within 30 miles of Wells Cathedral to be named as Cheddar cheese.

While the gorge's rock faces are challenging for climbers there are residents who find the climbs relatively easy: feral goats who were introduced thirty years ago to keep scrub down after the cessation of sheep grazing the area. Less amused by this introduction were some local property owners after having goats enter their gardens pruning flowers, shrubs, lawns and hedges. Nevertheless these sure-footed creatures are worth finding to photograph and watch.

I chose a day in early April before the holiday season started when Cheddar is overrun with tourists. After enjoying a light lunch at one of the many eateries with Yvonne we headed for the hills by driving up through the gorge to a point called Black Rock, to park beside the road. From here you can walk round either side of the gorge – even a complete circuit is possible. However we chose to walk the south east side, and with a rough climb we came out on the top to stupendous views over Somerset and the gorge. Would we see any goats was the next question? After ten minutes the answer appeared with the back of a very dark brown hairy animal appearing on the cliff edge. It was a nanny goat and by scooting round the edge of the gorge I found a second. While admittedly not being a dare devil, photographing the goats was not for the faint hearted. As at one point I looked down to find a sheer drop of hundreds of feet to the road below, with the cars looking like ants crawling along. Annoyingly over the far side of the gorge there were loud bleating noises coming from a large herd of goats, including a large billy goat which I dearly would have liked to photograph. Leaving the two nannies to their clifftop retreat we walked on for another ten minutes to be confronted by a large herd of goats including eight kids, five nannies and the chief of the herd, a striking billy.

Obviously quite used to people the goats took no notice of me. In return I gave them the respect of not straying too close. I was rewarded by the kids playing and Chief Billy resembling a 1970s hippy with his long hair, beard, chilled out and relaxing on the ground, as if he had consumed a bit too much wacky baccy. Of course I had to ask him to say '(Cheddar) CHEESE' before taking his photograph!

Little Pinky

On returning home after being away for six weeks, I found a message that had arrived from my friend Miranda saying, 'look what we have on the farm'. She attached an image of a hoopoe, a rare visitor to this country and a bird I've been wishing to photograph for years. Knowing the bird would only hang around for a few days if I was lucky, I drove to Miranda's farm near Carmarthen the next morning. Raining as it was, I had to witness this bird in the flesh (or should I rephrase that and say feathers). On arriving at the large Victorian farmhouse Miranda ushered me in for a cuppa. I received a nip on the leg from one of her two ankle-snapping terriers who were promptly demoted to another room, while they sniffed and barked at the door, determined to have a second chew at my bony leg. On draining my cup, Miranda took me outside to the slurry pit where the hoopoe had been seen. To her utmost despair there was nothing, not a feather

or a tweet, so we retreated back to the farmhouse. One marvellous farmhouse-made cake consumed and I made another sneaky trip to the slurry pit. There in all its splendour was the hoopoe with its pinkish colour it could not be missed. It was busy pulling grubs out of moist ground round the pit. I took a few record shots with the camera before backing off; the weather was so foul I knew I would not capture any impressive images with the bad light.

The following day's forecast was rain early morning clearing off by mid-morning to sun. Returning to the farm for once the forecast was right and the burning question was if the hoopoe was still in residence?

Peeking my head round the plastic-wrapped hay bales overlooking the smelly pit, there was no hoopoe, but still after travelling all this way it was a case of setting up hide beside pit and waiting. A rat scurried across the slurry and sat up below me having a clean.

I was thinking perhaps it was not the best idea to get my sandwiches out so I moved back beside the hay bales.

Within minutes my feathery pink friend turned up, pulling grubs out of the ground under a metal five-bar gate to my right and for the next three hours proceeded to appear and disappear in the same area. Using a 500mm lens with a 2X converter giving me 1000mm I was capturing good shots but not the detailed ones I desired. Miranda appeared beside the hide to see how I was getting on. I told her I would give it another half hour and call it a day and would come in for another tea and cake. No sooner had she disappeared when the magic happened. The hoopoe hopped away from the gate moving left across in front of me, the light was perfect, then it displayed, head feathers standing on end and feathers ruffled. It was the momentous moment to capture in a click of the camera!

Skomer Island, Puffin Metropolis

Visiting the puffin metropolis of Skomer Island off Pembrokeshire is a 'must do' for any follower of wildlife. Plan your visit well as you need good weather, otherwise the ferry from Martin's Haven won't run. A very early start is required as it's first come, first on the boat with limited daily trips. Last but certainly not least, there is no food or drink on the island so make sure you are well stocked.

For once I visited in May instead of my normal late June to see the mass of bluebells on the island and jolly glad I did for the sight was a sea of shimmering blue with some of the puffins playing with the plants in question.

The puffins' short breeding season running from roughly mid-May to mid-July is the only time puffins will be found on the island. Otherwise this cute little bird is at sea skimming across the waves, as it's not the best flyer in the world due to its wings being a compromise between flying and swimming.

My May visit also unveiled puffin behaviour I had not witnessed before. As puffins mate with the same partner every year, they seemed to spend a lot of time bonding, making their little comforting noises, fussing round each other before mating in front my camera, no sense of shyness here!

A later July visit would find the young known as pufflings in their underground burrows being fed by their parents. They seem to be continually flying back and forth to the sea catching mouthfuls of small fish and being constantly attacked by gulls for their tasty mouthfuls. If lucky enough to catch a glimpse of a puffling at an entrance of a burrow, it has none of its parents' colour just a ball of black fluff.

30

Muntjac Deer – Small, Cute, but Could be Trouble!

Brought to Woburn Park in 1900 the muntjac deer through escapees have spread throughout England and Wales. The size of a large dog, cute, shy and retiring but can be very destructive if gathered in numbers to trees, shrubs and rare plants. Muntjac are unusual compared to other deer as there is no annual rut and they give birth throughout the year. Sitting in my hide positioned on the edge of a New Forest woodland, two appeared to my right and gradually worked their way towards me feeding on thick foliage, coming within 6 feet.

Adders – Love with a Bite

Until recently I was always nervous of adders, inherited from my mother's sheer dread of snakes and my memory of nearly stepping on one while out walking with father when I was knee high! Now I find them fascinating, since being told about a south-facing earth bank that I now visit which turns out to be a breeding site abounding with dozens of these timid creatures. The lady living in the neighbouring house was left rather bemused after informing me that adders are regular visitors into her garden and that she lets her little dog out to bark at the reptiles to frighten them away; 'only one problem, their senses being scent, movement and vibration they have no hearing!' was my reply.

The end of March is their breeding season and the shedding of skin, swapping their darkened winter coat for a new, fresh and brighter spring fashion.

This is when you will find them enjoying the warm spring sunshine together as a loving couple. In this image on the right, the black and white male was curled up on the darker red/brown-coloured female when the male decided to yawn affording me the view of its fangs.

I never stop learning from my own observations and such was the case while photographing these two adders. Standing beside a single-track road with the two loving adders on the embankment I heard a faint rustle. Looking down a male adder slithered past my feet moving at quite a speed. Locals had told me they will travel quickly for some distance but I had never seen it for myself so I decided to follow this single male. I'm 6ft 1inch with quite long legs so if I describe the speed at which the snake was travelling as a slow walking pace it will give you some idea of how quick it actually was! Down the edge of the road it snaked, through a ditch over a cattle grid, past a farm gate then up a bank to a female adder curled up on a log. Obviously, it knew exactly where it was going. Quite how far it had travelled I have no idea except retracing the adder's route counted out as 78 of my long-legged paces and it had come from beyond where I had originally been standing!

With Gritty Ghoulies there is a Dolphin Ahoy

On my return to Wales after four weeks in Dorset I read reports of a friendly dolphin that had appeared in Poole Bay and was being regularly seen, often playing with jet skiers and following boats to the delight of many. Frustrated that I was now 180 miles away I thought my chance of photographing this magical form of nature would have passed me by. To my tremendous delight two weeks later I was back in Poole and the dolphin was still being frequently seen. From the information I had read this individual who had been named Danny was observed in the seas around Portland but had gone missing only to turn up at Swanage and Poole where it seemed to have found a new home travelling between the two coastal towns.

One location where the dolphin was being seen regularly was at the Sandbanks chain ferry, video filmed by a passenger early one morning on the crossing. This persuaded me to take a chance and catch the ferry from Sandbanks over to Studland and hope this exciting marine mammal would put in an appearance.

Yvonne came with me as we caught the bus from Poole to Studland village, via the Sandbanks ferry with no sign of the dolphin and the ferry crew confirming they had not seen it that morning. Disembarking the bus at Studland we made our way to the National Trust's Visitor Centre at Knoll Beach for a nice cup of tea and slice of cake before walking the beach towards the ferry in the hope we

Bottlenose Dolphin

might see something. It was a glorious day – the sort you dream about, blue sky, warm not too hot and we enjoyed the view to Old Harry Rocks round to the Isle of Wight. A section of the beach is for naturists, and well-marked by signs. Walking along the foreshore you have no option but to pass through the area. In the distance beyond the farthermost naturists' boundary I could see something orange but could not quite make out what it was! As we approached I was surprised to find it was a RNLI hovercraft on exercise from the nearby RNLI Headquarters in Poole. The crew on training appeared to be digging sandcastles, but on stopping to chat they told us they were digging out heaps of sand to form an obstacle course. The lifeboatmen who came from all over the country kindly showed us round the craft before advising us not to stand downwind while they practised zigzagging round the heaps of sand. Retreating to a safe upwind position, camera aimed to record this sight, the hovercraft's engines rumbled into life, its skirts inflating, the sand flying. I was glad of the advice to stand upwind. This tremendous noise caused intrigue from the naturists who popped up from the beach and sand dunes to look. I now know where the quote 'gritty ghoulies' originates from, and with sand flying, naked bodies dived for cover!

With what now appeared to be a 'naked' beach and the RNLI crew continuing to train, we walked on to the ferry with eyes firmly fixed on the sea, not a flipper or fin to be seen but I was hoping the hovercraft would come by as it would be nice to capture it on water. We boarded

the ferry and crossed to Sandbanks with no sight of Danny or the hovercraft, that is until we were about to disembark when in the distance coming around the headland came the hovercraft. Below, the ferry's car deck was becoming rapidly empty so Yvonne rushed to the ferry's ramp to get off while I stayed on the upper deck knowing that was the best location for taking photos. Below me cars were being loaded for the return trip but by now I was busy photographing the RNLI craft, before making a headlong dash to get off the ferry.

On meeting Yvonne beside the ferry ramp, she suddenly shouted, 'dolphin' and there was Danny playing around at the back of the ferry, before disappearing and resurfacing in front of the nearby Haven Hotel. After a few minutes two jet skis coming into harbour had the dolphin jumping out of the water and circling, while the jet skiers filmed it on their mobile phones. From my right the Poole to Swanage ferry called the *Solent Scene* was steaming out of harbour. As it passed I focused my lens on the bow wave in the hope that Danny just might appear and as if by magic he did! The passengers on the bow deck were looking at the horizon oblivious to what was swimming below, riding the bow wave. If only they knew!

Parakeets, Ultimate Lovebirds

The village of Studland in Dorset I have known since boyhood. I have spent many a summer's day on the beach with my parents and latterly it's a place I walk regularly and photograph except during the madness of school holidays when traffic queues prevail in whatever direction you travel. I also work with the area's main landowners, the National Trust, hence my wildlife knowledge for Studland I felt was fairly complete – smooth snakes, adders, sand lizards, deer, peregrines, otters, etc. However that theory was put to bed on meeting three members of the RSPB one day!

As I have explained many times before, a lot of my tip-offs about subjects to photograph come from talking to people I meet in my travels. Such was the case on meeting these three guys at Hartland Heath, near Wareham, Dorset. In fact we were having a bit of a post mortem as the weather was dull and grey with low cloud and had a depressing ambience not helped by the fact none of us had seen anything interesting all day. The chattiest of the trio had a strong Scottish accent. He explained they came from Winchester and belonged to the local RSPB group which was bit of a coincidence as I was booked to give a talk to their group the following month. We were discussing various birds and animals in the area when the word parakeets was mentioned followed by the location, Studland. 'What' I replied, trying to suppress the indication I was in fact flabbergasted. It's well known great numbers of this invasive species are around the London area and various other places but I honestly did not know that there were any in Dorset, a place I know so well – perhaps I'm becoming less observant in my old age or maybe complacent?

Next day, it might be a surprise to learn I visited Studland and within two minutes of walking with my partner Yvonne a bright green bird with pointed wings and making a squawking noise swooped over our heads. This confirmed they did exist although the weather was not good enough to photograph them. On visiting the Knoll Beach Visitor Centre where I know just about every National Trust employee, the general comment was, 'Oh they have been here years, did you not know?' 'Nooo grrrr' was about the only reply I could make!

Due to dull grey weather I had to wait a few days until I woke early one morning to bright sun, blue skies and no wind. A quick dash to the Sandbanks chain ferry over to the Studland peninsula was followed by the short drive to the village. On parking the car near the Bankes Arms pub it was a short walk. On the footpath I met an elderly lady walking her dog and as we walked together she asked what my purpose was. On telling her she exclaimed they were out and ready for me. So they were, six green beauties hanging from birch trees, nibbling branches in the early morning sun. Resting my camera and 500mm lens on the monopod I captured images in the wonderful early morning light. Although all looked good I needed something a bit special not a lone bird sat on a branch. Much to my joy one bird clambered up to another's branch and sidled up, obviously wanting a mutual preen. The feeling was reciprocated, which led to the pair of them acting completely soppy and daft, the ultimate lovebirds.

Spotted Woodpecker: a Chip off the Old Block

The sky was blue with the early morning gentle warmth of the rising spring sun with fog lying in the valleys below. I set off to walk part of the Epping Way which passes the front door of my house and runs around the circumference of the Sennybridge Army ranges. Heading east I wanted to check a small copse for woodpeckers and farther on a badger set I had not visited for three years. But my plans were thwarted by workmen with a digger clearing the ditches exactly where the woodpeckers resided.

Retracing my steps, I had walked only a short distance when a spotted woodpecker called and flew out of an oak tree beside the road. Inspecting the tree I found that a bough had snapped off and the woodpeckers had drilled a hole in the stump. Sticking a head out of the hole was a chick nearly fully grown and ready to fledge.

It was not the perfect place to photograph as ideally I would have set up my hide, but the tree was at the entrance to a farm so I decided that if I stood still for long enough the adult woodies would accept my presence and continue feeding their young. Within five minutes the female came in with a beak full of insects which were gratefully taken by a chick. She backed off for a moment and regurgitated up more food before moving back and was mobbed by a 'can I have more please' youngster. She flew off and within minutes the male came in with a quick offering which was eagerly grabbed. I stood there motionless for at least two hours watching the comings and goings. While the adults were away finding food there was non-stop calling from the ungrateful chicks, 'I'm hungry, I'm hungry!' It was noticeable that the hen woodpecker spent the most time feeding her offspring rather than the male. Due to there being only room for one chick to be at the hole at any one time I was unsure how many there were except for the sound of quarrelling coming from within the stump which confirmed there were at least two.

Black Grouse

How are an evening talk in Brosley, Shropshire and photographing black grouse on mountain in north Wales connected? With infinite wisdom I realised I could present the talk and then drive north for the grouse, sleeping in the car overnight ready for dawn and the grouse lek.

Cometh the day I headed off to Shropshire. The venue for the talk was close to Ironbridge, so I left early to visit the famous bridge. The evening talk to a W.I. group went well and on leaving the girls presented me with a large box of cakes for a midnight feast. The

grouse lekking was a wildlife spectacle I had never seen. Not only that but I was only too aware that it only happened at daybreak for about two hours and only in a location just off a small remote mountain road where they can be photographed from the car. The area is called World's End which sums up the areas' description to perfection. Luckily for me I know Iolo Williams the BBC's nature presenter who has been nothing but helpful towards my endeavours and knows the area well. Via email he had sent directions to a slight pull-in on a left bend before a slight rise in the road!

Arriving at Llangollen I picked up a single-track road which kept climbing with seriously sharp bends with verge drop-offs disappearing below me in the darkness. I passed a few lights shining through remote farmhouse windows before crossing a cattle grid and into complete blackness. Knowing this was the right road, I crept forward round blind corners, over humps, still climbing until the road flattened out then slowly dropped away down a long straight until I came to a sharp bend with a pull-in. If I had interpreted Iolo's instructions correctly I was there, taking the attitude that either I would wake up to what has been described as looking like black footballs or an empty playing field. Having arrived at 11.30pm I was tired and a good night's sleep was required as I had to drive straight back to Dorset the next day to present another talk. Parked on top of a mountain in April, it was freezing with no sleeping bag. I could not put the seat down to recline due to amount of presentation gear in the car, including a projector screen. It was the most uncomfortable night, the girl's cakes had disappeared by 1.30am

and from that point I drifted in and out of half slumbers.

I woke at 6.30am to strange calls – a noise I've never heard before only on the television, black grouse. My first thoughts were, 'I love you Iolo' (nothing romantic intended). With a Range Rover parked in front of my car and two behind, my thoughts turned to the hope that everyone would stay in their motors, as the grouse accept cars and are relaxed but they do not tolerate anyone getting out and will fly off never to be seen again that day.

Winding the car window down it was still too dark to photograph the birds whose constant calling alone was worth the wait on such a cold night, with more birds flying in out of the early morning gloom to join the calling throng.

The darkness slowly lifted to reveal a clear cold sunny morning and photographing could proceed, capturing the sight of twenty plus birds' constant posturing, gesturing, with the odd fight, the occasional quieting of display being aggravated by the fly-in of another potential rival which immediately seemed to stir all the birds into mass hysteria.

One bold grouse, or maybe just confused that the cars in some way were rivals, flew to the grassy verge and showed his display in all its splendour, calling, stomping round and jumping up and down as if on springs in front of the human spectators, before rushing off to challenge one of his counterparts.

At about 8.00am I noticed birds flying off at low level, one at a time and the noise becoming muted. By 8.30am all was silent with nearly all the birds gone, and this fantastic never to be forgotten sight was over. I must return one day!

Trail of the Lonesome Cuckoo

Living in a small Welsh village bordering the Crychan Forest and the Sennybridge Army ranges, with no shop or pub and the nearest of either a car journey of 20 miles away, it is a remote but beautiful place to self-isolate during a virus lockdown. The Coronavirus Lockdown had minimum impact as life here carried on more or less the same, with many employed within forestry work, a large farming community and with the recent addition of a fast mobile broadband signal others can now work from home.

Working as a wildlife photographer, spring is my favourite time of year. After the rawness of the winter months our wild world quite literally springs to life and for me nothing else indicates the start of the season more than hares boxing. I photograph this event every year on the rolling chalk down lands of Dorset and did so once again in March 2020. Two weeks into my endeavours, attempting to capture images of this enigmatic, mystic creature was brought to a sudden, dramatic halt by the Coronavirus Lockdown, which led to my hasty retreat back to Wales early the following morning.

Back in Wales during 'normal' times I can walk out of my door and rarely see anyone, only people working on the land or soldiers training. Now in lockdown with the absence of any military personnel, the wind was the only sound to be heard until the 14th April when an iconic sound echoed over the village, 'cuck-coo, cuck-coo, cuck-coo!'

I always set myself a goal to photograph a detailed image of a subject and the cuckoo was the perfect quest particularly as I missed a fantastic opportunity two years previously. While crawling on my hands and knees in the slow pursuit of a hare with my camera on the ground beside me, a cuckoo landed on a post no more than 3 metres away. Before I could react the bird took one look at me and took to flight, while I sank to the ground in surprise and frustration.

An adaptation of Laurel & Hardy's amusing song to 'Trail of the Lonesome Cuckoo' echoes through my mind as they are hardly seen in pairs and infamous for laying eggs in the nests of other species, for example dunnocks and meadow pipits for adoption by the unsuspecting parents.

On the morning of the 14th I set out to at least capture an image for the record and found the calling bird high in fir trees on the edge of a forestry block overlooking a cleared area. Entering the block some distance away I crept though the trees, placing my feet carefully so as not to make any noise to give my presence away while following the sound of the bird's call. After two hours of the cuckoo flitting about in the conifer trees, it came to perch far above my head and I captured my image. I always require quality images which means time, combined with luck. However I suffered several fruitless days mainly due to the wind robbing me of one of my main senses, hearing, which masked the direction of the cuckoo's call.

I do admit to becoming slightly obsessed with a subject to a worrying degree. Never more so than waking up one night at 3.15am and in my half sleepy slumber could swear I could still hear that cuckoo calling in the pitch-black night air. But I was not dreaming!!! Ten days into my search I struck lucky, being informed the cuckoo was heard that morning by two forestry workers planting by hand hundreds of conifers – a sight which would not look out of place in medieval times with bags of saplings on their backs and a spade in hand.

Walking down the hill from the hard-working men I heard a familiar call from a thin line of trees running parallel to the road into my village. Sneaking through the wood I found the cuckoo on the other side of a field flying off a fence into the boggy ground picking up grubs. Hiding behind a tree I captured good images of the cuckoo with lunch in beak. But I always push myself to capture better quality photographs. Whether I do snap 'THAT' image who knows. And what you may ask happens when the time comes when the cuckoo falls silent without success? As it happens, on warm summer evenings with my window open I can lie in bed and hear the churring noises made by nightjars, another must capture image!

SUMOR

Sumor, according to James Wilson's, *Dialect in the New Forest* (1913) is the pronunciation if you had not already guessed, for summer!

When I no longer wake to the sound of the blackbird singing outside my bedroom window and the cuckoo is silenced, it's the sign that the heat of summer has hit our shores. After the full-on proceedings of spring both myself and our wildlife tend to slow down, and take a much-needed sojourn.

Truth is when the temperature rises and the field crops turn brown it's too hot for many creatures. They try to find whatever shade possible to attempt to keep cool, so head for water whether a pond, river, lake or sea as all life requires that wet stuff. The young are starting to make their own way in life away from the reins of their loving parents. It's a good time to see kingfishers with their second brood of fledglings, and if lucky you may see otters and egrets. Away from the water, the early morning when the sun is gently warming the land is a good time to find reptiles sunning themselves before the heat becomes too great for their body temperature, or the cool of evening when owls, badgers, foxes pop out to enjoy the fresh twilight air.

My ideal summer day photographing is sitting on a river bank watching life float past, closing my eyes listening to the gentle tinkling sound of the water and enjoying the warmth on my back. If all is quiet, time for a snooze. Sometimes the day out is more important than taking photographs, but if a creature puts in an appearance it can only make the day perfectly, perfect!!!!

It's also the time of year to visit and sometimes exhibit at the many agricultural shows dotted throughout the UK so although I might be slightly quieter on the photographic front it is the time to show my work. In this way I have met so many people and by doing so I had my break into television by meeting Dr Rhys Jones star of BBC's *Rhys Jones Wildlife Patrol* when he visited my stand. Truth is you never know who you might be chatting to: from the little Welsh mountain sheep farmer whose yearly holiday to the Royal Welsh Show is the highlight of his year; to school children excitedly asking questions about my photographs; and OAPs reciting past memories. With such a vast range of people, they all have a life story to tell.

Bad Hare Day (Leveret)

On a glorious June morning just after sunrise, with barn owls the subject of my early morning quest flying from a barn on the skyline, the long down land grass was soaking wet with overnight dew. Suddenly this leveret hopped out onto the rough track before running towards me, as I was trudging along under the weight of photographic gear.

Throwing the gear off my back and sinking to my knees my camera was raised at the ready. The little hare, sopping wet and with a Galium Aparine (otherwise known as a Sticky Willy or goose grass) pod stuck in its fur above the left eye, stopped and sat looking at me only 3 metres away. Snap, snap, snap, went my camera. Being young and not wary of the possible dangers in this world, the leveret suddenly got up and sprinted down to my right knee before once again sitting down and looking longingly up at me. Coming to the rightful decision that perhaps I was not his Father, he tottered off.

Hares with stunning facial markings are the super models of the UK's wildlife. For the past eight years I have photographed the Jean Shrimptons of this hare world fighting off the David Baileys wishing to have their wicked way with her (hare boxing is the female fighting off the male's attentions). However, to this day I still have not captured the dream photograph I have lodged in my imagination which would be close up and in detail of two hares boxing face to face, standing on back legs, their bodies forming an upside-down heart shape.

56

A Rude Awakening

Being able to photograph on a working farm brings me back to the gritty roots of life. Were it not for farmers we would not eat. Also a good many of them have an interest in wildlife on their land such as Richard and his son Nigel who allow me to wander on the family's farmland.

With a genuine concern for wildlife, they actively encourage birds and animals to thrive including the siting of a barn owl box in the barn where the large round hay bales are stored. It came to pass that Nigel collected bales with his tractor at eight every morning, loading them onto a trailer. While this routine was carried out, one of the owls always came out of the box to hunt until Nigel trundled down the rough track and disappeared – obviously a rude awakening for the owl.

By accident I found the barn owl hunting one June morning at about 8.30am in the field behind the barn. Quickly erecting my hide and sliding inside I captured this image. It came about by the owl silently floating around the sky just 4 metres above the long grass – occasionally stopping and hovering, watching any movement below, sometimes flying on, on other occasions diving down into the wet greenery to capture a vole. Once it dived down and disappeared except for the wingtips just showing above the crop. Knowing it was the case of waiting for it to take off I focused the camera on the wingtips, watching for the slightest twitch informing me of an impending flight.

Suffering Pot Holes

The photographs shown here were taken in the month of June by sneaking up to within 3 metres of three hares and a leveret. How did I manage that would be a reasonable question, so here is your answer!

Hares can be very nervous at the best of times and make off at just the sight of you maybe hundreds of metres away. However by using a not so cunning plan I managed to squeeze myself and my hide through a hedgerow into a field containing six hares spread around some distance away, with a group of what appeared to be three off to my right.

After sitting watching for two hours and fighting a battle with overwhelming sleepiness and losing, I became drowsily aware of movement to my right: hares boxing. At the same time a little pair of ears popped up out of the grass, a little leveret. A feeling of 'must photograph' quickly forced out any remaining dregs of doziness.

Too far away to capture detail, I needed to somehow close the gap while still inside my hide so I picked it up shuffling along not trying to trip over while watching the hares at the same time. It became blindingly obvious that they were watching my movements. This was not surprising as I can only be described as looking like a

camouflaged dalek with two big feet, enough to frighten anything. I stopped, place my hide down and let my harey quest once again settle down. The time was about mid-day, the local church clock striking on the hour. Observing hares for so many years I have found they very often have a siesta about that time of day. Two of the three hares eventually disappeared below the grass line having a nap, with no sign of the leveret behind the one remaining hare to be seen – its mother laid out but not flat to the ground on lookout duty. I sneaked out under my hide and in a crouching position holding the camera mounted on a monopod walked arrow straight at the mother hare. To my surprise and delight there was no sign of movement from Mum. Creeping to within maybe 15 metres before I felt I was pushing my luck, I sat down in the field legs straight in front holding my monopod between my legs. There I sat for what must have been an hour. Besides a hare occasionally getting up, readjusting their sleeping arrangements and slumping back down, all was peaceful. Even Mum eventually rolled over on her side and disappeared. If you can imagine me sitting on the ground but now inching forward by placing the base of the monopod forward a few inches between my legs, supporting myself with my right hand and hanging onto the camera with my left hand, forward I moved. Two hours later I was within 3 metres. Mum by that time had sat back up but was quite content with her eyes closed. The hare to my left was flat but did pop up a couple of times to have a look; the hare to my right although by now chewing on grass simply was not bothered. The leveret, the sole subject of this quest remained in hiding, except for the tips of its ears. Suffering pain and torture from sitting on sharp flints and a sore hand from taking the weight of my body, I simply sat there in disbelief that I was so close, yet no hare was bothered.

As yet I had not taken any photos, worried about the clicking from the camera disturbing my furry friends, but the point of all this was to photograph. After a few snicks of the camera, everyone was still lying about having sweet dreams until eventually a hare to my left got up and decided something was not quite right. It stretched and went up to Mum who received a nudge and instinctively went up on her back legs and gave whom I presume was Dad a clip round the ear. Behind Mum, junior had now for the first time popped up to see what the fuss was about so I concentrated my attentions on the baby of the family, who had a stretch before sitting watching its misbehaving parents. The right-hand hare by now had also come into the fray and for a moment they all sat looking at me. I was kind of thinking how nice it would be if they charged at me, instead of which they sauntered off to the hedge before disappearing.

That evening was payback time for me with a cut hand and a bottom that resembled a pot-holed road surface, but the old phrase is 'No pain no gain'.

Garden Hogs

A secretive little creature hiding away in so many gardens is the dear little hedgehog, much loved although struggling through loss of habitat and many killed attempting to cross our busy roads. It's nice where possible to leave an untouched patch in your garden for wildlife in general but particular for the hedgehog. Always check under a bonfire before lighting as you could find one curled up underneath. If you do find one in the open it won't run away but will just simply curl up on sensing any danger. If you are a patient person just lie down quietly and given time the little cutie will relax and unfurl in front of your very eyes.

Cheep Thrills

How many of you have been at home and could declare you could hear a noise but could not find the source?

 I have to spend countless hours chained to the computer and that results in consuming many cups of tea while staring at the screen. Due to human nature, that results in regular visits upstairs to the bathroom and on doing so this particular day I could hear cheeping. On checking bedrooms and bathroom several times no form of life was to be found and I came to the conclusion the noise was from outside the bathroom window as every time I searched the noise stopped. Come bath time that evening I could still hear this noise which again stopped on entering the bathroom. The difference this time was that when I shut the door, behind it sat a rather beleaguered fledgling goldfinch. Finding the dear little bird quite unhurt I took a couple of photos before taking it to the garden and letting it fly off the palm of my hand into the great outdoors, hopefully to its parents.

Adult Goldfinch

Mink or Man, Guilty or Not Guilty?

For the past fourteen years I have spent many hours of pleasure sitting on the banks of the mighty River Tywi or Towy in Wales photographing all the normal culprits you would expect to see, herons, otters, egrets, kingfishers etc.

Flowing from its source in the Cambrian Mountains, it is dammed at Llyn Brianne before meandering through the Carmarthenshire countryside (as seen in the photograph), reaching the sea, the estuary guarded by Llansteffan Castle.

Always a great favourite with fishermen – indeed the largest fish ever taken on a rod and line in Britain was a massive 176kg sturgeon caught at Nantgaredig in 1932 – the river is good for catches of salmon, sea trout known locally as sewin, trout, eels, pike and lampreys.

What I call my patch has always been the upper waters of this great river from Llangadog to its source. With great sadness I have witnessed a huge downturn in river life during the past six years.

What exactly is going on here I'm continually asking myself. I confess to certainly not being a scientist, so the following thoughts are from my own humble observations and from talking to locals.

Six years ago, there were daily sightings of herons and egrets. I rarely see them now. A good reason for this is that fish stocks have drastically fallen. A local farmer commented about the river just above Llandovery, how it used to be full of fish; staring into the water as we chatted it was bare of any movement. A member of the local fishery association blames the problems on the Llyn Brianne Dam, flushing freezing cold water down the river with a such a dramatic sudden drop in water temperature that it was killing the fish.

Is the dumping of powdered limestone into the upper waters supposedly to counteract the effects of acidification cause by acid rain and extensive conifer forestation perhaps another factor?

With the current focus on plastic polluting the world I have witnessed farmers' plastic wrapping nearly encasing a fallen tree in the river and I have also seen video evidence of a farmer over spraying effluent into the river.

Just above Llangadog Bridge the river has changed its course due to massive rainfall washing everything away, river banks, trees. Is climate change the problem as without doubt the seasons are changing.

To my untrained eye all the aforementioned add up to the demise of river life. However one major factor not yet mentioned is mink, as here in Wales they are largely uncontrolled.

During the summer months when the water level is low, I can sit in my hide on a stone bank in the middle of the river and can nearly guarantee to see mink working feverishly along the river bank, investigating every nook and cranny, taking every living thing in sight.

In complete contrast I spend a lot of time on the River Stour in Dorset which is full of life where gamekeepers and fishery wardens trap mink. We have to consider one rivers' source is from chalk down lands the other from mountains which might make the difference. But it's for you the reader to perhaps draw your own conclusions. There is one common denominator which is man: we are the guilty ones, the cause of nearly all the problems; equally we are the ones who could rectify the situation.

Predator, the Mink

Fledgling Peregrines

In all my years of working with all types of wildlife, Midsummer's Day 2017 is perhaps the most exciting adrenaline-inducing day I have experienced, certainly one never to be forgotten.

A few days previously I had been walking the Dorset coastal footpath with Yvonne, when I heard the unmistakable sound of a peregrine calling a high-pitch wa wa wa wa. There beside the path a peregrine fledgling sat in its robes of youth.

A golden find which never lasts more than a few days in nature before the young birds make their own way in life, so as a photographer you have to grasp that time with two hands.

The following two days were the weekend. This is a time I never sit photographing in a public place as I'm forever being asked by passers-by what I'm photographing: besides disturbing me, this also disturbs my subject. However the following Monday I was on duty as usual. Two days of these beautiful birds sitting on the rocky cliff face all round me – with fantastic weather and glorious scenery – this could not get any better, could it?

Wednesday, Midsummer's Day, rising out of bed too early to take notice of the time, I arrived at the nearby car park before sun rise. Walking out to the headland I passed a beach party, girls skinny dipping, everyone waiting to celebrate the sun making its appearance as a globe peeking over the horizon. Stopping to take a few photographs of the red glow in the sky gaining brightness I walked on to the cliff arriving in time to see the dawn of the Longest Day. Sitting on the edge of a sheer drop is not the location to be if of a nervous disposition but there for yet another day four peregrine fledglings with parents perched, occasionally swapping their rocky viewpoints. As the sun rose above me the sea took on new life with boats of all shapes and sizes cruising past and two ferries loaded with passengers making their way to France and the Channel Islands. Life was good.

The next two hours were passed soaking in this scene, when zoom, a dark shape passed by my head at great speed: it was one of the fledglings using the updraft from the cliff face. Then a second appeared and rose up to tangle with the first, hanging on to its tail feathers before both fell out of the sky parting just 10 metres from the water below. All four of the young peregrines in pairs spent the morning practicing their hunting skills on each other, one moment passing by my head the next second miles away trying to evade their stalker or chasing their pretend prey.

I had to sit down on the cliff edge as there was real danger that if I stood trying to capture this whirling spectacle, swinging the camera round, I could have easily fallen over the precipice in excitement.

Sitting there with my feet only 0.5 metres from the cliff edge one of the birds flew up unseen from under my sight line. For a split second a pair of talons appeared between my feet, hanging on to the chalky edge, followed by a body that squawked with surprise at the sight of my size 11s before falling off backwards in the direction it had appeared.

Cursing the camera many times for it not focusing quickly enough, of course it was the sheer speed of these magnificent birds travelling at times at 100 to 170 mph which meant that even modern camera gear could not adjust the focus sufficiently speedily to keep up with nature. Sheer persistence on my behalf and a lot of luck meant I captured the photographs shown here.

Fledgling Peregrine

Time for Fun

Nothing signifies fun more than fox cubs playing. It's one of nature's most amusing sights, when old enough to explore the local surroundings, they roam picking up objects and having friendly fights with brothers and sisters to gain possession of them. This seems to be one of their main pleasures in life.

These photographs were taken in Poole, Dorset, where a friend had invited me to photograph the foxes who are permanent garden residents. The difference this particular year was that one of the naughty foxes started collecting shoes, obviously stolen from nearby properties. Just one of a pair was duly found in my friend's garden nearly every morning for three weeks. In the end there were so many, stolen shoes ranging from slippers to boots (and one boxing glove) which were hung from the front fence for people to claim them back. There must have been much scratching of heads by people in the area puzzled as to what had happened to their shoes!

I think at best you can describe foxes as collector maniacs: baking trays, tins, anything shiny and as seen in one of the photographs what appears to be a plastic flowerpot which was much prized.

That is the town fox but the country fox will not differ except for the items that are picked up. I've witnessed three cubs playing with a mouse, playing chase, stealing off each other while the vixen tiring of the cubs' antics picks the mouse up and lies down with it to stop the cubs playing. This might last for a couple of minutes before one of the youngsters rushes in and steals the dead rodent back and the game starts all over again.

Walk On By, Sand Lizards

Finding some forms of wildlife can be most frustrating, a feeling I'm only too familiar with. Mention such species as Welsh pine martens, polecats, even the smooth snake to be found in Dorset and I might roll my eyes and throw arms up into the air with frustration. One of the gems of Studland in Dorset is the rare sand lizard and it can be hard to find. Followers of wildlife will spend countless hours searching the wonderful heathland and sand dunes mostly without finding anything as noted by the National Trust who own and manage the area. It was to my amusement that during a meeting at the Studland National Trust Office one of the wardens told me about a sand lizard site just outside the office. Lo and behold sunbathing sand lizards on a raised traffic island in one of the busiest car parks, whilst droves of day trippers were walking by struggling with picnics and all the normal beach paraphilia.

I returned next day to the site, resigned to the fact that being the height of the holiday season with hundreds of people passing I would be driven mad by countless enquiries about what was I photographing. Fact, it's fatal due to people's curiousity or being just plain nosey parkers that man with camera, long lens attached, kneeling on top of traffic island draws attention. Actually I can be photographing in the middle of nowhere and someone appears asking 'what are you photographing?' to which I have to reply 'nothing now you have just frightened it off, grrrrrrr!'.

Maybe the public could sense the bad karma if I was disturbed as not one person stopped, not even to look, only two unbothered National Trust wardens in passing asked 'sand lizards?' to which I nodded confirmation.

The lizards I'm sure must be laughing at us while sunbathing in plain sight, watching all the comings and goings; bold enough not to move unless sat upon by an unsuspecting human.

A Smart Velvet Coat

I guess most fellas strive to try to look smart for their ladies for a special occasion. I have to say the thought of a velvet coat reminds me of the '70s, velvet jackets with big lapels, combined with bell bottom trousers with massive hems being the cool fashion of the time. I now shudder at the thought of wearing such gear, although luckily enough I never had a photograph taken for evidence. This proved to be a blessing in disguise as my mother always had to pull out old cringe-worthy photographs to show any new girlfriend I took home well into my fifties.

Both the red deer (yes, a white red deer!) in the photos are a different matter, looking smart with their antlers reaching maximum growth covered with a velvet coat which either falls or is rubbed off to reveal their stunning head gear in readiness for the autumn rut.

Ghostly in looks, a 'white' red deer in velvet

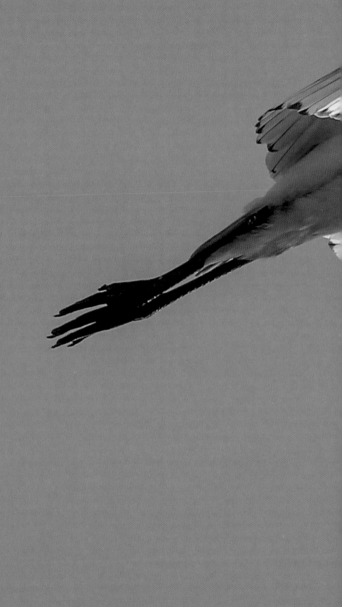

Spoonbills

Holding the perfect pose resembling ballerinas wearing classical tutus, perhaps waiting to dance *Swan Lake*, the striking spoonbills are now becoming a more common sight around the UK's coastal waters.

Watch its movements when searching for food, sweeping that monster of a bill from side to side occasionally throwing the head back after capturing a tasty morsel scooped up from the mud. In flight it's positively graceful, long wingbeats with neck outstretched as is the head with light showing through its beak and wings. It reminds me of the much-missed Concorde which was so purposeful and poised but alas now extinct except in museums along with the dodo, western black rhinoceros and more species than I dare think about.

Not so many years ago the sighting of a spoony would have had Twitchers clutching their binos rushing to the bird's location from all over the country to tick off their 'must see' list.

Believed to have become extinct in the UK during the 1700s due to habitat change and hunting it was not until the mid-1990s that spoonbills were recorded to have nested and produced young once again in the east of England.

To me this resembles the coming of the egret which was another not-to-be-seen avian only a few decades ago, remembering my first sighting while driving past old disused watercress beds in the Wiltshire village of Bowerchalke. Now the egret is to be seen on just about every waterway. To my way of thinking this has to be the ongoing climate and habitat change. For some species the change is beyond their physical capabilities, but others are thriving. Thankfully spoonbills are in the latter category.

Spoonbill, graceful in flight as Concorde

Darting Dartford

It is a long time since I photographed a rare Dartford warbler and thought it time to make a long overdue return visit to the location on the heaths of south Dorset where it resides. A secretive little bird normally heard before being seen, it darts from one gorse bush to another normally flying through the gaps between the gorse rather than any higher.

On arriving at a heath well known to me I carefully made my way through knee high heather watching for snakes warming in the early morning sun until I reached a thick patchwork of gorse. This had for some unknown reason a 3-metre diameter clearing right in the middle to which I forced my way through, receiving, scrapes and scratches for my troubles from the gorse's ridged sharp needles.

I had no option but to stand, for if I sat down I would not see the little bird as it flew so low. With the 500mm lens and 2X convertor attached to my camera which was then mounted on a mono pod for support I was ready for the long wait! It was desperately hot due to unbroken sunshine at the beginning of August. Although occasionally the split-second movement of a dark-coloured little bird caught my eye, which I recognised as a Dartford, that was all I saw all morning. Not capturing any photographs, I packed up at lunchtime to return the following morning. Thankfully day two was slightly cooler and my patience was rewarded by a Dartford perching on a thorn bush in full view. This proves the point, with my work you only get out what you put in which is time and luck!

HAERFEST

Haerfest, the Old English name for autumn.

It's appropriate to describe the season of autumn by the old English name of Haerfest as that is exactly what so many living creatures do, gathering up food to survive the long cold winter months. Birds decided millennia ago it was better to head for a winter break in a warmer climate and that it is time to depart.

Give or take a few days from 1st September ospreys leave for Africa, after spending six months on our shores. After arriving in March they nearly immediately mate, the eggs hatching in late April. Normally rearing two or three chicks they fledge only two or three weeks before starting the migration to Africa. Intense activity around the nest in the days before migration, with all the family present one day, the next gone, with maybe a bewildered youngster left behind for a few days wondering what had become of its clan! The fledglings fly on their own as the parents would have left without their offspring. It is one of the wonders of nature, how do they navigate, indeed even know where to go and in the case of the parents, return year after year to the same nest?

Haerfest means red squirrels are busy gathering up nuts, acorns and such like then safely storing them away mainly by burying in the ground, ready to be once again found and cracked open for a winter's Sunday lunch. I can't help thinking they remind me of Gabriel Oak from Thomas Hardy's novel *Far from the Madding Crowd*, rushing round making sure the harvest is safe from the approaching storm. Meanwhile others resemble the drunken farm workers chasing each other up and down, round and round the trees oblivious to any danger, while I am sure there is a Sargent Troy high up in his drey wondering why Bathsheba was helping Gabriel. For those of you familiar with this beautiful but in many ways tragic masterpiece of a novel wondering what happened to Farmer Boldwood, he was a grey squirrel and was always an outsider!

While many a creature disappears for the winter others reappear. Some birds migrate for instance from the north to our shores escaping minus-stupid temperatures, while other residents although never leaving these shores were just well hidden during the summer months such as cranes. These gangly birds suddenly appear flying in great numbers during September after the summer of rearing young in the deep Somerset reedbeds. These are either on private land or in conservation areas affording these rare birds (in the UK) protection. From my own observation (and disappointingly it's not a bird I can spend day after day watching), the best time to see them is at daybreak. Seemingly the cranes ground roost on one site and take off flying to another site to spend the daylight hours, I suspect feeding. It's worth a million bars of gold to watch them, nay, to listen to, their haunting calls in the stillness of dawn with mist rising off the water meadows. Close your eyes and imagine the ghost of the Knight of Avalon riding a white steed through the reed beds, to throw a deep chill down your spine. As if frightened by the sight of this charging knight the birds rise up in a grey cloud, with massive slow wingbeats they circle as if still half asleep trying to find their bearings before heading off westward, their calls disappearing as the light of day grows brighter.

The magnificent beast of the forest appears at this time of the year on the fighting grounds of the open heathland. The red deer stags who spend the rest of the year leading a singular existence spread out across a large area which can be in some areas restricted by human occupation, now gather. Three weeks of my calendar year is firmly marked (do not double book!) to allow uninterrupted early morning visits to the New Forest. The peak of the red deer rut I have noted in my diary for the area seems to be around 18th October. That differs in other parts of the UK by only a few days although weather conditions play their part: the ideal is hard cold frosts that last on into the morning. Similar to the call of the cranes, the sound of stags bellowing, echoing across the land, in the early morning dawn gives the feeling of something primeval. It's the sound of natural raw power, the opposite to the sounds heard in spring which are of love!

Less than a week after the red rut peaks the fallow deer rut also reaches its climax. The male bucks seem to gather in much larger numbers than the red stags and are more sociable except when it comes to the rights of mating with the girls.

I have encountered both red and fallow at unexpected close quarters. If asked which worries me the most the fallow wins hands down as on two separate occasions in particular fallow bucks put the fear of god into me. In the first instance I was watching a herd from several hundred metres away when a doe broke from the herd followed on its heels by a buck. I was sitting on the ground with my back against a tree looking over 3-foot-high fern. The doe could have run in any direction but no, it ran straight at me over the green then into the fern. Halting within 2 metres of where I resided, and startled by my presence, it darted up the hill to my right. A few seconds later her suitor arrived, breathless. I looked up, he looked down. His hot breath I could feel warming my face (with very bad breath!) as his nostrils were within inches. Dare I say it but I thought the end was nigh. However the thought of his good time girl overruled any thoughts of dealing with a quivering cameraman and off he shot up the hill. The second occasion I was sitting in my hide. The buck had made its stand (mark where to fight from) on top of a flat-topped hill in thick wood, so rather than disturb the deer I set up my hide at the bottom of the hill and settled down to see what if indeed anything would happen. Several hours passed. Not being able to see the proceedings on top of the hill I could only go by noise, obviously a lot of grunting, hoofs running about and squeaking from the does being chased. After a while all went quiet and down the hill in front my hide appeared Mr Masterful in all his prime. The girls in his life had run away so he had come down looking, hence the problem as the only thing he found was my pop-up hide and he did not like it one bit. I rested my camera on my knees as I did not want to upset him even more by taking photos. I can assure you I know what it is like to receive a stare with intent and the feeling of being helpless as I was at his mercy.

At only 5 metres away he was scraping at the ground with his feet, grunting, bellowing, ready at any minute to charge with his mighty antlers. Without any reason he turned away and walked off. Was it just a show of strength? Whatever it's not an understatement to say I was relieved!

Whirling Dervishes

The sight of a white buck is rare so when I came across one of these beauties chasing his does about during the rutting season, he quickly became the focus of my attention. His forest patch was in thick undergrowth at the edge of a small clearing at the bottom of a slight hill. He only made a brief appearance when chasing after a mistress into the clearing before disappearing again. His position was given away by bellowing, however, and every now and again a reply bellow echoed down from the brow of the hill behind me from another buck hidden in a thickly wooded plantation.

While I was waiting to capture an image, the white buck suddenly broke cover and charged up the slope to one side of me heading towards the bellowing of the second buck somewhere behind me on top of the hill. Before I had time to think about my next move, the sounds of clash, whack, crack reached my ears. The boys were fighting. Grabbing my camera I ran up the hill to find the most ferocious fight, antlers locked, the bucks spinning round in combat. The rutting is very intense and a huge physical strain so its maybe two minutes of fighting is followed by a quick break of maybe thirty seconds to catch their breath and to eye up the opponent before continuing their struggle. During their breaks they either stop with antlers locked, heads down watching each other (I can see the whites of their eyes), or with antlers unlocked they bring their heads up to catch breath, watching each other. Neither will take a step backwards as it would be seen by the opponent as weakness. Once again they lower heads and lock antlers with such force one might just have an antler break.

All their strength is directed through the neck. That's why heads are carried low and the power comes from the hind legs through a straight back into the neck. If the neck is turned the power is lost and the opponent has the advantage.

The fight took place in an area sparse of trees but those trees remaining gave me enough cover to follow the fight, darting from tree to tree while the two whirling dervishes span round and round, locked in battle.

After half an hour of brute effort the pair broke off their struggle and strolled side by side down a fire track into the distance as if they were old friends.

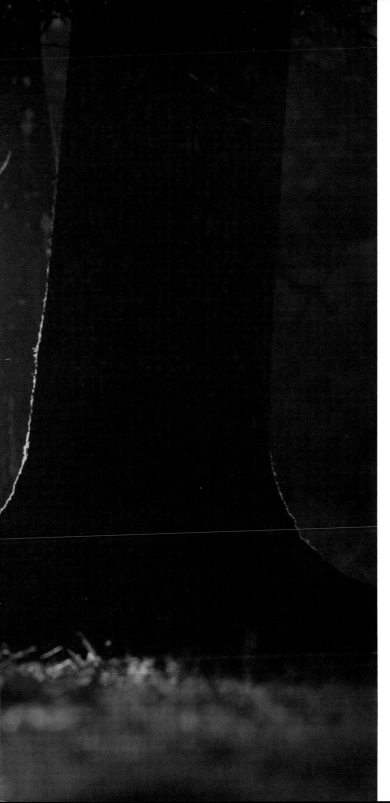

The Beauty of Dawn

With a rich crop of fallen acorns the fallow deer gather to eat under the clump of oak trees in the middle of the heath. It's also the centre of their rut with many numbers of bucks in the same location fighting over a limited number of does.

Arriving at the edge of the heath just before daybreak I dumped all my gear in some fern before crawling with camera in hand into position, lying flat on the ground behind a small oak tree. Fighting ebbed and flowed in and out of the oaks still too dark to photograph. Does followed by bucks broke off in small numbers disappearing into the forest until just the one buck remained, bellowing, wondering where his fellow deer had disappeared. The sun rose gently above the tree line causing me to curse as it was directly in front of my position, blinding my sight of the buck, until that one moment happened: the buck framed by the trees in the new golden light of day stood and bellowed, my image capturing his hot breath in the cool morning air.

The Royal Family

One lovely day during the red deer rutting season I happened across a Royal stag with about thirty hinds. Two more stags were on the periphery of the group trying to approach the girls but being chased off by the beautiful Royal. They were on the edge of a heath but gently without rush moved into the thick wooded forest where I decided to track them. I have found red deer are very nervous on open heath but in wood are much more relaxed, maybe because they feel more secure? I simply walked slowly at their pace parallel to the group some 15 metres away while they ate branches, chased around and generally chilled out. I did not want to disturb them, just taking the occasional photo; they could see me but did not care about my presence. After an hour it was my lunch time, and tummy rumbling I walked some distance ahead of the group and sat down on a tree trunk to eat and drink. After five to ten minutes the deer caught me up and enveloped me in their midst. It was one of those never to be forgotten moments in my life. It was not a time for taking photos as the click of the camera would have disturbed them and brought the wrath of the Royal down on me, as at one point he was just 5 metres away, giving me just the occasional glance. The hinds were sedate being subject to the occasional harassment from one of the three stags as they moved on gently, flowing past like a wave that parted in front of me and closed behind. Maybe I should have felt apprehensive but instead I felt the opposite, completely calm. I truly believe animals can pick up on this, which maybe is a good thing as when I thought the whole group had passed, on rising from my perch and walking off about 20 metres round a thicket I came truly face to face with one of the stags, not the ideal situation. Exposed to this stag I was at his mercy. Don't panic Mr Mainwaring comes to mind; the worst thing anyone could do would be panic and run. I simply stood still for a minute then slowly backed off. He could see I was not a threat and went on his way to catch up the other reds.

Black and White Photography

It was while I was exhibiting during the month of September at the National Trust's Knoll Beach Visitor Centre in Dorset that one of the workers there said he had seen a stork flying over Corfe Castle. He was still insistent after intensive quizzing and doubts voice by me as to it being a heron or something equally similar! It was not until the next day that the Trust's Wildlife Officer for the area, Kevin, told me there was a stork, one of a group released in Sussex two months previously. Not only that but Kevin also told me the location in a field outside Wareham.

Early the next morning I found myself just outside the old Dorset town. Walking a footpath across a field to one end of a pond with horses dotted in this and the adjoining fields, I spied the stork at the far of

the pond. With no access from the footpath I walked to neighbouring heathland and found another pond and there quite undisturbed was once again the stork who had moved. Being a cloudless early morning, the light was perfect and coming from behind me gently lighting up my subject. But photographing a black and white bird on its own makes the most soulless of pictures, so I desperately required some type of prop to make the image interesting. That's when something trotted into my life and my camera's eyepiece namely a black and white horse. You can capture a perfect photograph of, for example, a kingfisher sitting on a post but a far better and more interesting image would be a kingfisher with a fish. In this case a black and white stork and horse!

Dipper

It's nearly guaranteed that if I spend a day beside any river in Wales a little black and white bird will appear: the enigmatic dipper, rare in much of the UK. An industrial, hardworking bird, never seemingly stopping to rest, working along the shallow waters at the edge of the river; or in summer when the flow of water decreases it will fly out to any rocks showing either just above or below the waterline, diving into the water to take small fish, larvae and invertebrates. The name dipper comes from the bird's constant dipping motion, bobbing up and down as it seeks food. Due to its extreme focus on searching for food my presence sitting quietly on the riverbank does not distract or disturb this understated bird.

It is worth noting that any animal or bird that is mainly black in colour is difficult to photograph with any real contrast or detail. Good light is certainly required but not too harsh. For this image it was early morning, with a sunny clear sky allowing a soft bright light which brought out what colour there was in the feathers; even so there is slight burnout on the white bib. For those of you into photography and not to bore everyone else I will quickly mention I nearly always use JPEG files, the same format as used on compact cameras, mobile phones etc. Having said that on my cameras I have the option to use RAW files. With JPEG you lose a small amount of content and hence detail. RAW files are exactly that, and with no loss of detail the content is as taken and seen by the camera in a raw state which allows the images to be enhanced which is more than useful for instance in the case of photographing badgers when the light is fading (which is the only time I use RAW in adverse light conditions).

Legged-it

One evening on a short autumn break away in Cornwall myself and Yvonne found ourselves in the pretty harbour town of St Ives. After enjoying a tasty seafood dish in one of the many quayside restaurants we strolled round the harbour wall and there on top of the stony breakwater was a small flock of turnstones. These very pretty unassuming little birds were so accustomed to people they just sat and looked at us while I photographed from only 0.5 metres away using a short lens. Yvonne noticed many were standing on only one leg. Nothing unusual about that you would assume, a little bird resting, except there was another very good reason they stood in such a pose: on investigating we found only one leg did many possess! Hopping around on one leg did not impede their ability to dive in and nab any chips that passers-by threw their way before their nemesis the villainous gulls arrived. As found at all seaside towns, the gulls were bossing around other members of the feathered community. My theory of the turnstones' misfortune would be that these wicked birds were perhaps responsible for the amputations?

Frustrating Times

During my time living in Wales my overriding quest has been to photograph a Welsh pine marten. With many unsuccessful attempts I thought my luck had changed when an offer by Paul Harry who had been capturing truly wonderful HD film footage using camera traps offered help.

Paul took me to a remote, wooded, steep-sided valley and explained that he had found the martens use fallen trees as bridges to run along. With a bit of detective work we identified one such tree with the moss scraped back, a sign that indeed our quarry had been visited. With camera traps set out and primed to capture any action the next thing was to put out something rather tasty to lure the martens in. It was then Paul extracted boiled eggs and strawberry jam out of his bag.

Leaving two eggs and lashings of jam smeared round the tree we departed with the plan to return a week later to check the cameras to see if there had been visitors. Except I could not wait that long and returned the next day to find eggs and jam gone and not one but two pine martens had been filmed. Excited by such a quick positive result I had with me more jam and eggs which were duly left and once again checked the next day to find consumed with just one marten captured on film. So for the next four weeks myself and Paul made it on site at least every other day to place out food and finding regular visits by one or two martens.

The pine martens never hung around for long, more often than not picking up an egg, sometimes dropping it on the ground and having a game of football with it, dribbling better than Georgie Best before making off into the darkness. The jam though seems to be their favourite morsel as sometimes I sat an egg in a lump of jam and watched footage of the martens trying to lick the jam away under the egg rather than take the egg first!

Unlike Paul who uses different techniques with cameras and lights being activated by motion sensors, my way is to be there in person to press the shutter release myself. It's much more difficult as the marten is nocturnal and rarely seen in daylight.

Having pine marten visiting nearly every night I made the decision to reserve one week of nights to spend in my hide with a camera and flash being operated using a remote handset, the camera being set at a fixed focal length and screwed to a bracket close to the fallen tree.

In the days before the planned week it took me a while to double check and test camera settings in my garden then two hours on site setting camera focal length and brackets before adventuring out on the first evening. One big damper (quite literally) ended my plans! The weather during the preceding weeks had not been perfect but passable – after all this was October. But coinciding with my planned week it all changed with the forecast of rain predicted to arrive the first night around 10.00pm. I had arrived on site at 4.30pm with the remnants of daylight to set up equipment and snuggled down in my hide ready for the long night. Heaven forbid that I ever lose my hearing as it's so important to me. Sitting there during the darkening evening the nocturnal world came alive, foxes screaming, owls calling and other unknown inhabitants of the wood making their presence known to friends and rivals. For me on the other hand I had to be as quiet as possible. Dropping a spoon onto my metal thermos sounded like an explosion in the still night air. You can't help but to keep checking the time 8, 9, 9.30pm still no movement on the fallen tree, then the sound of a drip on the hide roof followed quickly by more regular, drip, drops! I dived out of the hide and gathered up my camera gear which is not waterproof and shovelled it into protective bags just in the nick of time as the heavens opened. It was the Welsh equivalent of a monsoon.

I had to admit defeat for the evening, packed everything up and loaded down with bags of gear I walked sometimes knee deep in water for half an hour back to my car, by then soaked even though I was wearing waterproof clothes.

For the whole week it rained with no respite, and with my work taking me away for several weeks that was my missed chance for the year. The two martens in question having now moved on, question is will I ever capture an image of a Welsh pine marten? Watch this space!

Trail camera pine marten footage.

IN WINTER TIEM

James Wilson's, *Dialect in the New Forest* (1913), the pronunciation for 'in winter tiem' meaning 'in the wintertime'.

A winter's dawn has that clean, unblemished feel about it, which draws me out into the stark fields and woods. All around the world is stripped of its green clothes, left shivering in its naked form and the animal world if not sleeping is fighting to survive, all of which I unashamedly admit to love.

The little red squirrel is resplendent in its winter coat complete with ear tufts which it loses during the summer. The starling murmuration swirls in the sky. Hundreds of thousands of birds arrive on our saltmarshes. What is there not to enjoy. Perhaps the cold is the largest unwelcome factor at this time of year. I may look as though I've been inflated with a bicycle pump, with so many layers worn, but to stay warm is the critical factor as there is nothing worse than having an event happen in front of the camera lens when signal from brain won't meet digit to press shutter button.

I would sooner be out walking with the camera during this season than sitting in a hide for pretty obvious reasons. I mainly concentrate on birdlife as we have such a wide range to photograph in the UK during the winter with many visitors flying in to our comparatively mild climate to spend their winter months. Although the winter of 2019/20 was mild I noticed many birds who regularly visit southern UK did not arrive or in much fewer numbers than normal. Is this going to become more regular due to climate change? I do admit to watching social media for bird sightings and through that I have made friends with people of the same interest and we help one another.

It's also a busy time for me travelling around the countryside giving talks with slideshows which is something I love to do, describing my work to various nature loving groups, which allows me to visit new areas and wildlife species. At the talks I never know who I maybe talking to, or indeed who I may meet and hear their stories. Very often I'm tipped off about something rare although more often than not a photograph is placed before me of a species I could die to photograph, accompanied by a remark 'oh yes we had it here for several weeks but it's gone now'. I have to reply through a faint smile hiding gritted teeth, 'oh how lovely'!

Frozen in Time

I always wished to capture an image of a hare in snow ever since the day I was walking the Epping Way in mid Wales. Fighting driving snow I came to a gate and was fumbling with my frozen hands to open the latch when a lovely brown hare ran up the fence line towards me before veering off and disappearing into the whiteout. A few years later in Dorset it snowed, and with my 4X4 I made my way to my friendly farmer's estate on the high down lands. Parking in the farmyard I strapped on my back all my gear and waded through knee high snow to a hedgerow at the highest point of the downs. I find hares very often run along hedges so I positioned my hide under the bare hedgerow, crawled inside and waited. To this day I can state it's the coldest I've ever been in my life, the strong raw wind cut though any gap of clothing worn. After four hours I must have passed through the state of hypothermia, my body uncontrollably shaking to such a degree that if I wore false teeth they would have fallen out with the chattering of my jawbone. Attempting to hold the camera was sheer pain and trying to steady it was impossible, so when a brown furry hare kicking up snow while travelling at high speed across the frozen tundra appeared, it took all my mental powers of concentration to take required images. Normally I would be over the moon at having captured images equivalent to winning the World Cup but I fear it felt like scoring an own goal being so utterly frozen. In time it was all I could manage to extract myself from the hide, pack everything up, trudge 2 miles back to car and spend the rest of day removing icicles from places no human should ever have them hanging!

Bandit in the Reeds

I would like to meet the person responsible for the naming of the bearded tit as I fear this is a mistaken identity as anyone who has been lucky enough to encounter this most beautiful member of the tit family would surely agree.

A Mexican bandit would be proud to own such a moustache as found on this little bird, wearing a sombrero, playing a guitar and serenading his senora when not robbing a bank. A more fitting name would be the bandit tit.

My journey to 'bandit country' took me to the RSPB Radipole Reserve, Weymouth, Dorset which must be considered as one of the best urban reserves in the UK. Surrounded by roads and to one side a row of stores, car parks and a train station, with the main footpath running through the reserve spurring off in a couple of directions at the northern end, it's well used by locals going about their daily business. Leisurely walks can be had, through the head height reed beds surrounding Radipole Lake, fed by the River Wey, flowing into the sea via Weymouth Harbour.

I had two previous visits to Radipole to look for bandits, the days being windy and cold, conditions which do not suit this little bird although the reserve has a multitude of estuary bird life and Marsh Harriers which are seen most days. On my third visit I arrived at sunrise on a clear, cloudless and windless January day and walked the reserve listening to the calls of the inhabitants waking from their chilly slumbers. With the sun slowing rising about the town's rooftops I met Paul and Sharon walking the footpath. Having never met before we started chatting and as they were regular Radipole visitors I quizzed them about the best vantage points to see the tits. Two locations were noted and also the fact the 'beardies' would not appear until the temperature rose. Having been so kind to arm me with information the helpful couple strolled off down the path while I took my time, peering into the reed beds and listening for the distinct 'pinging' call of the tits. Half an hour later 'pinging, pinginggg', was to be heard and to my delight not one but a posse of eight bandits flew into the reeds 10 metres away, lightly fluttering from reed to reed, taking seeds from the heads. At times it was almost although they were playing with each other. With only one bird hanging from the top of a reed it was bending but very often a second

bird would land on the same head which would cause the reed to bend over to the ground and both birds falling off.

Disappointingly the birds were in thick reed so I could not obtain a clear shot and also the sun was behind the birds which meant I was trying to photograph into the sun, not ideal for capturing a close quality image. I was in two minds to move but did not want to lose my quarry, when to my right came Sharon, running and waving her arms to attract my attention, before arriving breathless and blurting out (if I had not guessed by then) that they had 'beardies' beside the path 200 metres away. Gathering up my gear we trotted down the path, took a right turn and found Paul with a bearded tit 4 foot away, perfectly lit in the sun, busy dissecting the head of a bulrush. With such generosity shown by Paul and Sharon and the fact I had my 500mm lens with a 2X extender attached I was capturing fantastic detailed images.

The bearded tit shown left never did walk the same again!

Pere David Deer

Pere David, what are they? Or is it a place many ask, having never heard the name let alone seen one!

I always have a feeling they are the forgotten deer of this planet: they very nearly became extinct only a few decades ago. However they are a remarkable story of survival and the only subject in this book photographed in a park.

China is the native country for the Pere David. In the nineteenth century the only remaining herd resided in the Nan Haizi walled hunting garden belonging to Tongzhi, Emperor of China until 1895 when a flood demolished a wall. Most escaped to be killed by starving locals leaving about thirty remaining. Troops fighting in the Boxer Rebellion (1900) killed and ate the remaining deer making them virtually extinct.

The deer were named after a missionary called Pere David who made the western world aware of their existence. A small number of deer had been transported to zoo collections in Europe prior to the rebellion. After their near demise, Woburn Park launched a successful breeding programme, collecting deer from the European zoos. More recently during the past thirty years Pere Davids have been reintroduced back into China and are once again breeding well in their native country with the reintroduction programme ongoing.

Besides Woburn, Pere David can be found at Whipsnade, Margam and Knowsley. Their coat is grey during winter, reddish during summer, with the tines of their antlers facing backwards. Unusually they shed antlers twice a year with the summer set being the largest, timely for their May/June rut; and a smaller winter set which very often do not grow.

I find everything about this fascinating deer very different to our native species. Notably if there is a disagreement between individuals they will box – imagine overgrown hares, up on back legs striking out with front, real handbags at dawn stuff.

My location for photographing the Pere David has been Margam Park, south Wales, where one winter I witnessed three fully antlered red deer stags mixing with the Pere David, wearing their grey uniforms in beautiful contrast.

Crossbills

Countless times have I quoted that local residents are people who you listen to for their knowledge of the area and wildlife. Such was a classic case in managing to photograph these crossbills.

I had been booked to present a talk at a nature reserve in Dorset bordering the New Forest. A few days prior to the event I had noticed outstanding images of crossbills on social media taken in the New Forest. On the day of the talk people starting arriving including one of the reserve wardens, a girl called Jackie, proudly cuddling her little bridge camera asking me to have a look at the screen on the rear of the camera to preview images she had taken a few days ago. To my surprise, they were the very same crossbill images I had seen on the internet.

Explaining to her how jealous I was and would kill to capture such images she described where to park in the Forest and the rough directions. One guess as to where I headed the next day!

Quite honestly the Forest is a large expanse and although I tracked down the area I could not pinpoint the exact spot and there was also the possibility the birds could have moved on. With four hours spent walking with regular stops to look and listen, my patience gone, it was time to relent with the mindset that I would not be photographing this fairly rare and unusual bird with its crossed-up beak used to prise pinecones apart.

Two days later I received an e-mail from Jackie who exclaimed excitedly she had revisited the area and the birds were still there. Would I like to meet up and she would guide me to the site? The following day we met in the Forest car park, Jackie with her dear little camera, myself with Canon camera body with walloping big lens attached. Rather like little and large we made our way over the heathland and up a slight hill before descending the other side where Jackie suddenly stopped and whispered euphorically that she could hear the crossbills. We stood still, waited and listened. No more than five minutes later a cock bird which had a reddish tinge to its appearance flew to the top of a tree in front of where we stood and starting singing. A few minutes later another cock bird flew into the same tree and perched lower down the tree followed by a hen bird easily identified by a green appearance to its plumage, both within a distance to capture detailed images. For a good hour Mr Cheerful perched on the pinnacle of the tree and sang his jovial song while the couple below hopped from perch to perch nibbling away at the tree and taking the occasional flight to earth, before returning to the safety of their wooden branches.

My belief in local knowledge once more proved reliable. Nevertheless luck plays a deft hand, as my site return the subsequent morning proved, as it was void of crossbills!

Kestrel

I had been visiting Portland Harbour, the site of the 2012 Sailing Olympics, on a cold windy December day walking round the harbour walls hoping to see with no success one of the three bottlenose dolphins who had made the old Royal Navy base their home.

On driving back over the Chesil Causeway to my right I noticed a kestrel hunting but with restricted parking I could not stop until I reached the car park by the Wildlife Trust's Visitor Centre. Hurried payment at the ticket machine was followed by swift assembly of camera with 500mm lens before crossing the busy road. There was a strong north wind so I knew by walking south towards the point I had seen the bird, we should in theory meet as the kestrel would be flying into the wind to hunt. This of course depended on the bird still seeking prey and not breaking off to take a rest, but within five minutes I could see a small black dot in the sky. As I continued walking and the kestrel hunting, the gap between us closed, the dot became larger to seemingly grow wings, then a tail before the detail of colours and markings became apparent to the naked eye. Two problems I had to overcome. First I wanted detailed images so I stopped and fitted a 2X convertor to my camera giving me 1000mm. Second problem and more difficult to overcome was the sun, as walking south with the bird hovering in front of me the sun was behind my subject rendering it just a black shape in any images I may try to capture. Somehow, I had to work my way round the bird to position the sun behind me and get the light with little or no shadows on my subject without frightening the beautiful bird. Gradually and very slowly I walked past the hovering bird when it swooped down close to me hovering just 2 metres off the ground. For a split-second the light was perfect, that was all I required, snap went my camera!

Winter Fox

We all need a nice warm place to curl up during the winter. However the fox has not the luxury of a nice log fire or central heating, so the chance to relax in the sun during the deep mid-winter is always taken. The bank outside Yvonne's house during January is bathed in early afternoon sun and this fox has its sunbed under a fir tree, hardly raising an eyebrow to watch passers-by and oh, so photogenic.

Hawfinches

Some may say that it is slightly creepy hanging out around graveyards in the short dark days of winter with cameras. But I would like to think that the land's permanent occupants can appreciate the beautiful birds hopping about above their heads, namely hawfinches.

Why graveyards? Most traditional churches in the UK have yew trees believed to have been planted for the making of the famous English longbow, with historical records documenting the use of the longbow in the Hundred Years War 1337-1453. During winter months the hawfinches feed on yew tree berries, simple!

Stop Cock (Queen) King

In my mind, without question Lymington Salt Marshes is the best coastal nature reserve in the Hampshire area. You can walk for miles, with views across the Solent, boats of all shapes and sizes sploshing about their business, with exceptional bird life to be seen.

My quest on this particular visit was spoonbills, walking miles from one end of the reserve to the other trying to catch up with five that flew overhead, only to land far far away in never never land in terms of capturing detailed images before disappearing altogether somewhere in the expanse of marsh.

On my return trek on an embankment I came across three people surrounding a lady in a wheelchair, politely saying hello as I passed without receiving a reply – their attention taken by something much more interesting than myself, perched on a wheel of a cast iron stop cock used to control water level.

A lovely looking female kingfisher, easy to identify by the redness on her lower bill (think of it wearing lipstick, the male's lower bill is black).

The kingfisher sat like a statue before diving off into the water catching a tasty meal, returning to its man-made perch to devour its fishy supper, repeating the performance time after time quite unperturbed by the human spectators.

I captured some superb images, while the look of joy in the faces of the onlookers was priceless.

Murmuration

From the heavens the black cloud descended and hung above their heads, jibbering loudly, before falling to the limbs of this earth for darkness to envelop.

Why do starlings murmurate? During winter months the gathering of huge numbers at sunset form clouds of large billowing black shapes in the rapidly demising daylight, before falling earthwards to roost in the arms of trees with the thunderous sound of their chattering. There are many theories, the favourite being safety in numbers from predators. However for once, it would be nice for nature to keep its secret!

124

Playtime at the Reserve, Reflecting on my Schooldays!

A winter's morning photographing birds on a nature reserve, watching the comings and goings of the avian characters, brought back memories of myself and old school friends playing (and otherwise) in the secondary school yard.

Lesser Yellowlegs

This rare little bird I found searching for food in the mud round the extremities of the lake, singular in nature, keeping clear of the multitude of birds, mixing only occasionally with a few ruff.

Lesser yellowlegs would be the type of name my fellow school inmates would so kindly call me, due to my legs resembling a chicken's (not improved over the years) sticking out from underneath my school shorts. I am also very singular in nature, never one to mix with the multitude.

128

Ruff

Gathered together in little groups, another wader with its long legs and slim pointy beak ideal for foraging in mud and foliage.

Wearing the uninspiring battleship grey school uniform with flecks of brown, was Joan, attractive, tall, slim, long legs with a slightly pointy nose, surrounded with an aura of 'you can look but not talk and certainly never touch me', always hanging out with two or three friends.

Moorhen

Black in colour with a few traces of white on wings and tail with an outstanding red and yellow beak, it seems to have a very twitchy nervous disposition, walking and running around with jerky movements.

Raymond, son of a coalman, his uniform was always black, it was originally grey but now ingrained with coal dust, a timid lad always seen running at speed with a bright red face.

Lapwing Otherwise Known as Peewit

In bright sunlight the lapwing shows a colourful shimmering plumage crowned with a crests. Seen in large numbers over wetlands and farmland, it can be heard making its call, peee-wit, peee-wit, and is fantastic to watch in flight, very aerobatic – a proper show-off.

Nicknamed 'The Cheeseman', who always wore the latest clothes and strutted his stuff, stamping into the school hall for morning assembly wearing shoes with steel heels indenting the wooden floor, showing-off, much to the despair of the caretaker. It was impossible to ignore his presence – the girls flocked round him at playtime.

Marsh Harrier

Hundreds of birds suddenly rising into the air in panic gave a clue of foreboding: low over the reed beds the justification of their terror glided, a marsh harrier, eyes fixed searching for its next victim.

Children were playing and laughing. Suddenly all sounds of happiness subsided, replaced by the noises of running feet as many tried hiding away. With high wire fencing surrounding the school playground there was no escape – Gaffer the school bully had emerged from yet another spell in detention. My yellowlegs quivered in fright hoping his steely gaze would not notice timid me and steal my sweets.

NOTE: For my own well-being, fellow schoolers names have been changed!

Roe Deer by Name, Bambi by Nature

If there is one species of deer in the UK I consider as a true embodiment of Bambi, it is the roe – simply as it never runs but leaps, it truly bounds. Most deer are twitchy at the best of times, however I believe that the roe are possibly the most nervous, making off with huge bounding leaps on noticing anything slightly different. On occasions I have been sitting quietly in my camouflaged hide set back in a hedge with other species calmly passing by, but not the roe who normally appear by passing through or leaping over a hedge and on taking one look in my direction they retreat in their hurried manner.

Robust creatures as they are, I had a very 'dear' encounter with one many years ago while driving my old mark one Ford Escort along a narrow country lane late at night. A roe jumped the roadside hedge and landed on the front of the car writing it off. The deer staggered around obviously in shock and disappeared into the darkness. I reported the incident to the local gamekeeper, but thankfully no injured or deceased deer was ever found. The possible explanation for this deer's lucky escape was my car's inbuilt crumple zone. Due to the cheap materials used in car manufacturing during that period of time most cars suffered rust which on impact crumples!

Ratties

Love or – as most people do – hate them, with the exception of a children's favourite called Roland, rats feature in all our lives, never far away living a secretive life of scavenging.

Many years ago, while living in Hampshire, the garden shed and garage became infested with rats. Consequently the rat man was summoned. I will never forget simply because he had a larger than normal nose; taking one sniff of the air he exclaimed 'I can smell em'!

According to my learned friend they will travel miles, are great communicators and breed better than the proverbial rabbit. Unfortunately they carry Weil's disease, will chew through just about anything including electrical wiring insulation, are known to take the odd chicken and cause numerous other problems. I first came aware of Weil's in 1971 when my father told me of a local Rockbourne farmer, Timothy Olivier (a relative of the famous actor Sir Lawrence) passing away due to catching this disease. Because of this I always make sure hands are well washed having been in the vicinity of any rats.

I'm quite used to seeing rodents as my father worked in an animal feed mill all his life with the exception of being called up for National Service. As a child every Saturday morning I used to play in the mill jumping about on the sacks of grain with feral cats roaming catching the furry critters. My father used to open the mill at 7.00am all year round, crank up the huge old Crossley heavy oil engine and start it via compressed air. As it rumbled into rotation the mill used to come alive as the machinery in all five floors was run off this one engine via shafts and flat belt pulleys. His routine was to start the engine on the ground floor, charge upstairs to check all the machinery was running and that no flat belts were slipping which could and did cause fires, and which had the potential of explosion due to grain dust. One dark morning Dad fired up the engine and, running up the stairs to the first floor in half darkness, he nearly reached the top when a rat came scurrying down followed by large feral cat. The cat jumped off the top of the stairs and hit Dad firmly in the chest nearly knocking him over beside receiving a huge fright!

My own overwhelming memory of rats was while working for an agricultural engineering firm and some of the work undertaken was in animal feed mills. Working on site at a Dorset farm the mill building was divided in half with a conveyer travelling through a square hatch connecting the halves. Being a typical youth and too lazy to walk round from one half of the building to the other I took the short cut poking my head through the hatch and started crawling through. On hands and knees with front half of body through hatch I found rats hanging above my head from the flap-type door and running underneath my body between my hands and legs, I came out of that hatchway quicker than the Eurostar train exiting the Chunnel.

More recently I had visited a reserve to successfully photograph a rare bird. There I found hordes of rats due to visitors putting down bird food which the rats consumed with great delight. Maybe it's me being weird but I find them quite intriguing, bold and very photogenic. Like naughty children the rats were feeding on the low walls of a little concrete bridge where a lady had put bird food. First a scouting rat emerged from a hole in the end of the parapet and with jerky nervous shuffling movements, warily came onto the bridge. The slightest movement from me sent it scurrying back to the hole for a few seconds, repeating the performance before becoming convinced I was not a threat. Eventually another rat appeared, then another, yet another until I had ten rats before me, some in pairs feeding some alone. Then a passer-by approached and the rodents scattered in different directions into their holes, waiting until the possible danger had passed, before repeating the performance yet again appearing from their hideaways.

Seaside Capers

Have you ever visited the seaside determined to get your toes wet? Off come shoes, hitch up skirt or roll up trouser legs and rush into the water's edge only to run out again before an incoming wave soaks you. I suggest a name for this behaviour could be, 'sanderling'!

Sanderlings are members of the sandpiper family and are one of my favourite birds to watch during the winter, the name coming from Old English, sand-yrolling, 'sand-ploughman'. A hyperactive visitor from Arctic breeding grounds, they can be found in small flocks spending their time avoiding the waves scampering back and forth feeding on crustaceans, worms and insects.

Waxwings

A welcome sight in this particular season of short days was the arrival of waxwings from Scandinavia arriving in numbers in the south of England.

It's a winter visitor to our shores normally to be found in Scotland, the north and east of England. However this year its southerly arrival was due to a large population and shortage of food consisting of berries in its normal feeding grounds forcing the birds further afield looking for food.

A striking and beautiful-looking bird it gives me the impression it has been painted. The markings are simply glorious, with its crest black facial markings, black wings and with white, red and yellow tips to wings and tail it's easy to see how it has come by the name waxwing.

There had been sightings! Having never seen one let alone photographed one, my camera sights were set on capturing an image. 'Your mission (Dave) should you choose to accept it!' seemed quite a suitable phrase quoted, from the *Mission Impossible* films except I'm no Tom Cruise and the only fancy gadget I own is the camera. However I do have stealth.

Reading online reports of sightings, I headed for Corfe Mullen in Dorset, with no idea where I might find the waxwings if indeed they were still there. The large village consists of one very busy main road through the middle with large housing estates branching off on each side, a pub, a school and few shops, hence people everywhere, not my normal location for photographing wildlife.

The slight clue that I had found the birds was a gaggle of photographers beside the road in the village centre; either that or maybe Tom Cruise was there after all sleeping in the bedroom of the house opposite the paparazzi!

Parking the car around the corner I walked to join the frozen bunch wielding their long lenses only to find that I had met some a year before while photographing otters.

The photographers had been observing this pretty little bird for about a week. Seven birds in number, their day was spent flying from a high tree to our left (which was too far away and against the light to allow capturing any photographs), down to a bush covered in berries located in the front hedge of a property beside the road. The birds would only spend enough time in the bush to gorge themselves full before flying back up into the high tree for the next hour or two before repeating the process.

These short periods of feeding were the only chance to photograph. Fighting the other photographers for position, the weather was blowing a gale with quite heavy cloud with a few short breaks of sunshine and with the birds never quite perched in the right position. It was a very frustrating day, never quite capturing 'THAT' photograph. On the point of giving up, the sun came out for a longer length of time and the waxwings came down, whiz bang I got 'THE' photo of a waxwing with berry.

Meanwhile back at ground level it's surprising what a stir we were causing standing there with our camera gear, especially the long lenses. Cars slowing down, their occupants stopping to ask what we were doing, staring at us or trying to spot what we were trying to photograph while still driving along, with toots from infuriated van drivers cursing the slowing of traffic, I quite expected the arrival of police to move us on.

With time passing quickly the yearly cycle of seasons completed, once again we look to the future and new life.

ACKNOWLEDGEMENTS

I am forever in debt to the following people as without their friendship and support this book would not exist.

Neil and Gina Smith to whom I will be always grateful.

Dr Jane Goodall, PhD, DBE & UN Messenger of Peace.

The Jane Goodall Institute.

Dr Steve Etches MBE.

Mark Coleman.

The SDS Group.

Steven Pugsley and all the staff at Halsgrove Publishing.

Bill Oddie, Pete Sheppard, Mark Whitley, Iolo Williams, Ian Durham, Ann, Richard and Nigel Friend.

Peter Maidment and all the staff at National Trust Visitor Centre, Studland, Dorset.

The New Forest Heritage Centre.

Colin and Irene Preece, Alicia Leow-Dyke, James Byrne, The Welsh Wildlife Trust and Beaver Project.

As always, all the landowners who so kindly give me access to their land.

All the individuals (too many to list) for their help in finding species.

Bea who is much missed and always in my thoughts.

Above all Yvonne for her love, help and unrelenting support, this book is for you, with my love.

INDEX

SDS are **experts** in **managing** and **digitising** archives…

…for **now** and **future** prosperity

SDS Heritage (part of the SDS Group) are accomplished digital project managers of archives and a specialist scanning bureau. One of our core areas of expertise is in the handling and digitisation of rare and precious heritage documents. We use non-destructive techniques and equipment to digitise:

- diaries
- journals
- maps and plans
- notes and jottings
- papers
- photographs
- project work
- artworks

…and other such historical material. We process, index and curate these digital facsimiles into bespoke search and retrieval software solutions for private use and future research.

SDS Heritage has worked with some of the UK's finest and quirkiest institutes, establishments and private individuals over the last 25 years, preserving many valuable historic archives for online access.

…for **individuals, institutions, landowners** and **estates**

For more information, please contact Mark Coombes on **01202 496513** or e-mail **hello@sds-group.co.uk**

www.sds-group.co.uk
www.sds-heritage.co.uk

SCANNING SOLUTIONS AND IT DOCUMENT MANAGEMENT SYSTEMS SINCE 1994

sds group